GREAT WAR BRITAIN
KIDDERMINSTER
Remembering 1914–18

GREAT WAR BRITAIN

KIDDERMINSTER
Remembering 1914–18

SALLY DICKSON
With Moira Brown, Catherine Guest, Derek
McCabe, Sue Wood and Bill Wood, members
of Kidderminster & District Archaeological &
Historical Society

The
History
Press

To all the people of
Kidderminster
who lived or died during the Great War,
in appreciation of
the disruption they endured
and the efforts and sacrifices they made
on behalf of the nation.

First published 2014

The History Press
The Mill, Brimscombe Port
Stroud, Gloucestershire, GL5 2QG
www.thehistorypress.co.uk

British Library Cataloguing in Publication Data.
A catalogue record for this book is available from the British Library.

ISBN 978 0 7509 5210 1

Typesetting and origination by The History Press
Printed in Great Britain

CONTENTS

	Timeline	6
	Acknowledgements	9
	Introduction: Kidderminster on the Eve of War	11
1	Outbreak of War	28
2	Going to War	42
3	Work of War	70
4	News from the Front Line	98
5	Life at Home	122
6	Coming Home	148
	Postscript : Legacy	161
	Bibliography	173

TIMELINE

1914

28 June

Assassination of Archduke Franz Ferdinand in Sarajevo

4 August

Great Britain declares war on Germany

5 August

Aliens Restriction Act allows internment of enemy aliens

6 August

Paper money introduced – 10s and £1 notes

8 August

First Defence of the Realm Act (revised and extended many times)

23 August

Battle of Mons

6 September

First Battle of the Marne

16 October

Belgian refugees begin arriving in Kidderminster

1915

February

Volunteer Training Corps established in Kidderminster

25 April

Allied landing at Gallipoli

1 May

Kidderminster Special Constables established

7 May

Germans torpedo and sink the Lusitania

29 May

The Larches Red Cross Convalescent Hospital opened

9 June

Ministry of Munitions established

July

National Registration begins

15 December

Derby Scheme: all military-age men to attest by this date

1916

24 January

First Military Service Act introduces conscription and sets up Tribunals

31 January

Zeppelin over Kidderminster

21 February

Battle of Verdun

23 April

Battle of Katia – Worcestershire Yeomanry

21 May

Daylight Saving Time introduced

June

Kidderminster War Savings Association established

1 July

Battle of the Somme

27 August

Italy declares war on Germany

22 December

Ministry of Food established

1917

1 February

German U-boat offensive against trade shipping

6 April

The United States declares war on Germany

9 April

Battle of Arras

April

Food Campaign in Kidderminster

31 July

Third Battle of Ypres, known as Passchendaele

22 August

Local Food Control Committees established

20 November

Battle of Cambrai

December

Food rationing begins

1918

3 March

*Russia and the Central Powers
sign the Treaty of Brest-Litovsk*

21 March

German Offensives begin

8 August

*Hundred Days Allied
Offensive begins*

October

Flu epidemic reaches Kidderminster

11 November

*Armistice Day, cessation of hostilities on the
Western Front – conscription and tribunals
suspended, two-day bank holiday begins*

21 December

*Kidderminster's National
Kitchen opened*

1919

2 April

*1/7th Battalion Worcestershire
Regiment returns to Kidderminster*

28 June

Peace Treaty of Versailles

1922

22 October

*Dedication of Kidderminster
Town War Memorial*

ACKNOWLEDGEMENTS

Although this book has been compiled from a wide variety of sources, the researchers' special thanks are due to the Trustees, staff (past and present), and volunteers of the Museum of Carpet in Kidderminster who have made their archives freely available to us and whose help and support has been far in excess of what we might reasonably have expected.

In addition, we would like to thank the members, staff and volunteers (as appropriate) of the following organisations for facilitating the use of archives and books, for allowing us to make use of their researches and for publicising our own project: the Library of Birmingham, Library of Birmingham Botanical Gardens, Kidderminster Civic Society, Kidderminster Library, *Kidderminster Shuttle*, St Mary's Parish Church in Kidderminster, Warwick University Modern Records Centre, Worcestershire Archives and Archaeology, and Worcestershire Regimental Museum.

We also want to express our sincere appreciation of the way so many people have freely given of their knowledge and precious family archives for us to use in this book, including: Graeme Anton, Robert Barber, Graham Birley, Nigel Gilbert, Nicky Griffiths, Peggy Guest, Jacqueline Hartwell, Ruby Henderson, Kathryn Hughes, Mrs James, Andra Kleanthous, Francesca Llewellyn, Roger Matthews, Beryl Millichap, Bob and Phill Millward, Shirley Morgan, Francis Rainsford, Tom Roy, Peter, Judith and Karen Rawlins, John Roach, Melvyn Thompson, Mark Thursfield, Bryan Tolley, and Barbara Wilkinson (who we thank for her additional help).

In my capacity as author I would like to add a personal thank you to everyone, especially my family, friends and fellow members of KDAHS, who expressed interest and enthusiasm for the project and thereby nudged it towards completion.

If anyone has been omitted above it is a most regrettable error rather than a lack of appreciation of their contribution.

Note: Numbers in brackets refer to illustrations.

INTRODUCTION

KIDDERMINSTER ON THE EVE OF WAR

Although it lasted only four and a quarter years the 1914–18 Great War had a catastrophic effect on the nations involved, and still elicits a shudder of horror when it is mentioned 100 years later. The deaths and injuries caused by the fighting were beyond all imagining, and, for that reason, subsequent histories of the conflict have concentrated on the combatant forces.

However, this was 'total war', involving all sections of society. The young men went to fight. The non-combatant population provided the weapons, food, materials, care and moral support needed to keep the forces in the field. Nor were they immune to the fighting as their sons, husbands, brothers and sweethearts joined the lengthening casualty lists. In Britain, refugees from the combat zones were an ever-present reminder of what might happen if the fighting reached her shores. Preparations were made to defend them to the last. This book looks at the part Kidderminster played in this 'total war' and what it meant in practice for the people of this small north Worcestershire town.

In 1911, Kidderminster had a population approaching 28,000, most of whom (24,333) lived in the borough. This was a young population, with 80 per cent under 50 years old (Fact box 1). Some 20,000 people were of working age,

Fact box 1	
THE POPULATION OF KIDDERMINSTER IN 1911	
Male	
0–14 years	3,720
15–69 years	8,504
70 and over	405
Total	12,629
Female	
0–14 years	3,933
15–69 years	10,792
70 and over	572
Total	15,297
Total population	27,926

including 8,500 men. About half the total male population of Kidderminster at this time was eligible to fight before the war had ended (1).

Whilst the town was the centre of a road network stretching across neighbouring countryside to the towns of the Midlands and Welsh Borders, cars were not yet numerous and mainly the preserve of those who could afford chauffeurs. Nevertheless, a car manufacturer, the Castle Motor Company, was already established in the town, together with motor engineers, Leonard Wyer & Company. For the rest, buses, trams and trains were the main form of transport. The railway station, on the east side of the town, provided good links to Worcester, along the Severn Valley via Bewdley, and to Birmingham, where many local people worked. Trains were as important for the carriage of goods as they were for people. Trams went from the station to Stourport and the town's cabs were still horse drawn.

Other commercial transport ranged from horse drawn carts, through bicycles, motorcycles and steam-powered vehicles, to motor vans, and still included the canal. Businesses in the town

1. *Age structure of male population of Kidderminster in 1911. The dark bars indicate age groups eligible to fight at some time during the Great War.*

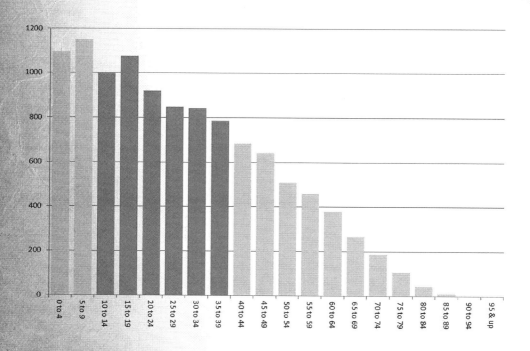

catered for most of them; saddlers, blacksmiths, shoeing smiths and horse breakers could all be found. There were also wheel-wrights and coach and carriage builders. Motorcycle agents, John Wright & Sons and Rhodes Brothers, both made motorcycles (2), while the Co-operative Engineering Company in Cherry Orchard dealt with steam traction.

On the eve of war Kidderminster was both an industrial town, dominated by the carpet industry, and a market town serving a substantial rural hinterland.

The carpet industry was the dominant employer in Kidderminster. There were over twenty manufacturing firms in the town, some specialised in yarn spinning or carpet making, and a few did both (Fact box 2). The owners and directors of these firms were the richest and most influen-tial men of the town. Reginald Seymour Brinton, educated at Winchester and Oxford, succeeded his father as chairman of Brinton's Carpets in 1914 (3). Already on the local council, he was mayor of Kidderminster for the first two years of the war and took a leading role in the governance of the town throughout the war.

2. Fred Wright, no.56, from John Wright & Sons, motorcycle agents in Blackwell Street. Here as part of the Abingdon Ecco Team for the 1914 Senior Tourist Trophy on the Isle of Man. He was to die in November 1918 from war wounds. (Carpet Museum Trust)

Michael Tomkinson, a locally educated man, and William Adam, from Paisley, went into partnership in 1869, making rugs. In 1878 they developed and patented the first powered Chenille Setting loom and purchased the British rights to the American Spool Axminster loom. They held the rights to both processes and controlled the licences. Tomkinson lived at Franche; he was an alderman on the town council and mayor of Kidderminster in the last two years of peace, and continued to be active in town governance and patronage during the war, even though he was then in his seventies. Other members of his family also made unselfish contributions to the war effort.

By 1914 Peter Adam, as head designer, had inherited his father's interest in the firm. He too had been mayor of the town for two years. He lived at 'Cairndhu' on the Birmingham Road, and opened the grounds for a variety of fundraising events during the war.

William Henry Stewart-Smith, a younger man in his thirties, was in charge of R. Smith & Sons, founded by his grandfather. Educated

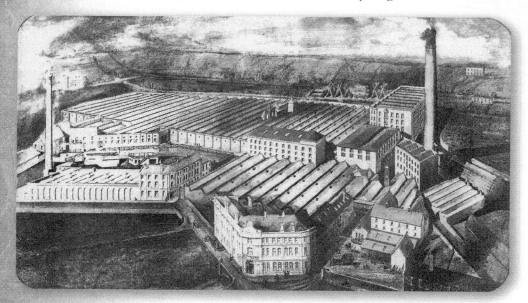

3. *Brinton's town centre carpet factory in 1911. The main office, built in 1876, is in the foreground. The factory was powered by a coal-fired stationary steam engine; the engine house projects above the north light weaving sheds towards the back of the factory. Brinton's Bull (see Chapter 5) was situated on top of the four-storey building between the engine house and the main office. Coal and bales of wool were delivered along the adjacent canal. (Kidderminster Library)*

at Malvern College and Cambridge, he was elected to the town council in 1911 and became president of the local Chamber of Commerce in 1916. He used his extensive energy for the war effort on the home front, and later saw active service.

The carpet firms provided about 40 per cent of the jobs in the town – in July 1914 Tomkinson & Adam employed nearly 1,500 and Brinton's employed well over 1,000. About three quarters of these employees were women, however it was the men who held the key weaving jobs. They started as 'creelers', maintaining the continuous supply of yarn into the backs of the looms, becoming weavers with their own looms at the age of 21. Women were also creelers, but in most factories they had no opportunity for promotion to weaver, although they were employed on other preparation and finishing processes. Only at Tomkinson & Adam were women employed as weavers on the lighter Axminster looms which were, arguably, outside the agreement with the Carpet Weavers' Association. After a visit from Mary Macarthur in 1912, a branch of her National Federation of Women Workers was established in the town.

There was a much smaller, but highly significant, iron industry in Kidderminster. The Stour Vale

---

Fact box 2

THE CARPET INDUSTRY IN KIDDERMINSTER

Yarn Spinners:
Edward Alfred Broome & Son, Castle Mills, New Road.
Greatwich, New Road.
Hoobrook Spinning Co., Hoobrook.
Kidderminster Spinning Co., Park Mills, New Road.
Lea, Slingfield Mills & The Sling.
Watson Brothers, Pike Mills, Green Street.

Yarn Spinners and Carpet Manufacturers:
Brinton's, Exchange Street.
T&A Naylor, Pike Mills, Green Street.

Carpet Manufacturers:
Broome & Brookes, Mill Street.
Chlidema, Green Street.
Carpet Manufacturing Company:
    Morton & Sons, New Road.
    Richard Smith & Sons, Mill Street, Brussell Street, Imperial Works & Park Wharf Mills.
Cooke Brothers, Worcester Cross Works, Oxford Street.
Empire, Foley Park Works.
Edward Hughes & Sons, Town Carpet Mills, Mill Street.
Jelleyman & Sons, Townshend Works, Puxton Lane.
Carpet Trades (Herbert Smith):
    Charles Harrison & Son, Long Meadow Mills, Dixon Street.
    James Humphries & Sons, Mill Street.
    Jason Skin & Rug, Dixon Street.
Frank Stone, Exchange Street.
Tomkinson & Adam, Church Street & Mount Pleasant.
Victoria, Green Street.
Woodward Grosvenor, Stour Vale Mills, Green Street & Worcester Cross.

Ironworks, to the north of the town, was owned by Baldwin's Ltd iron and steel business. An amalgamation of five companies in 1902, Baldwin's was flourishing by the outbreak of war. Stanley Baldwin, MP for his native town of Bewdley, was a director and deputy chairman of the company. His position, wealth, energy and social conscience all contributed to the war effort in Kidderminster as well as further afield. Other iron founders in the town were Herbert Bale at the Albion Foundry in Pitts Lane, John Russell whose foundry was in Oxford Street, and Bradley & Turton who had foundries at Clensmore and Caldwell. Prunell, Lamb & Co., engineers on Station Hill, did a lot of work on the looms and other machinery used in the carpet industry.

Kidderminster's MP, Eric Ayshford Knight, also came from a family that had originally made its money in the iron industry. His uncle, Sir Frederick Knight, had been lieutenant colonel of the Worcestershire Yeomanry, and he was major and commander of the same Territorial corps in 1912. He had been the town's MP since 1906.

Before the war there was one retail outlet in Kidderminster for every thirty people in its population, while nationally there was one outlet to fifty-nine people. The doubling of this density in Kidderminster reflects its position as a market town and suggests that its hinterland population equalled its own. The key shopping streets formed a rough cross (4). Shops ran in a line from the railway station down Comberton Hill, along Oxford Street and Vicar Street, through the Bull Ring and up Mill Street to the north-west of the town. High Street and Swan Street, occupying the historic market place and crowded with shops, led north-eastward off the main shopping axis and joined Blackwell Street and Coventry Street, also full of shops. On the opposite side of the main axis was another shopping street, Park Butts, continued by Bewdley Hill. Almost 390 shops were to be found in these streets. Thursdays and Saturdays were market days, when the town was especially crowded.

Most of the town's retail outlets were small specialist businesses, often sole traders (Fact box 3). Many were scattered through the suburbs of the town, convenient when most people walked to the shops and carried their purchases home, and when

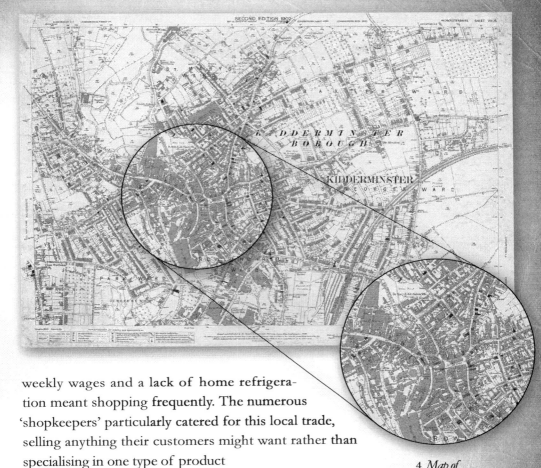

weekly wages and a lack of home refrigeration meant shopping frequently. The numerous 'shopkeepers' particularly catered for this local trade, selling anything their customers might want rather than specialising in one type of product

Details of one of these small business emerged when the proprietor, Henry Joseph Pretty, a butcher, was sued for breach of promise of marriage in March 1916. He was a butcher's assistant when, in 1912, his mother left him £75. He started his own butchery business with a mortgage and bought premises in Mill Street, including living accommodation, a slaughterhouse and shop, for £465. In 1915, his stock of meat cost him £3,500 which he sold at a mark-up of 10 per cent, giving him a gross profit of about £350. Out of this he had weekly shop expenses of about £5, including wages of £1 to his assistant and 13s 6d to a boy. He had developed a high-class business dealing with at least 150 pre-booked orders every Saturday. The £1 per week that Pretty claimed he was earning from the business was not enough to support a wife. The prosecution's estimate of £2 per week would have been sufficient.

4. Map of Kidderminster in 1902 – see page 160 for additional enlargement of the town centre. (Worcestershire Archives and Archaeology)

Fact box 3

RETAILERS IN KIDDERMINSTER ON THE EVE OF WAR

Food	
Butchers	44
Bakers & confectioners	51
Fried fish dealers	20
Greengrocers & fruiterers	30
Grocers	40
Milk dealers	10
Shopkeepers	123
Industrial Co-op branches	4
Other food	22
Public houses & beer retailers	126
Coal merchants & dealers	23
Clothing	
Tailors	22
Dressmakers	27
Milliners	20
Other clothing	32
Drapers	41
Newsagents	20
Tobacconists	16
Footwear	67
Hairdressers	35
Jewellers, clock & watchmakers/repairers	11
Refreshment rooms, etc.	12
Other	144
Total retailers	940

Nearly a quarter of the retail outlets in the town had female proprietors. As independent retailers they had the opportunity to earn the same as men, something they were rarely able to do as employees. They dominated the women's clothing trades, especially the dressmakers, milliners and wardrobe dealers. Many were shopkeepers, pub licensees and food retailers. There were no female hairdressers. Many were married, possibly widows who had taken over their husbands' businesses (5).

Shops stayed open late for the factory workers, and they offered another valuable service – credit. Customers' purchases were recorded in a book and the balances settled on paydays or when they could afford it. This was a major risk for the small shopkeeper.

A threat came from the shop chains that were beginning to find their way into Kidderminster. They bought in bulk, undercut the prices of the independent retailers and took prime positions in the town's main shopping streets. In the High Street were branches of the Maypole Dairy Company, Boots Cash Chemists, Freeman Hardy and Willis, two other boot makers, and three grocers' chains. The smaller independent retailers included a watchmaker and jeweller, an art needlework depot, drapers, a baker, a saddler, a stationer, and a tailor. The small chemists, boot and shoe makers and most of the grocers had to go elsewhere for their business, although Meredith Brothers were an exception, their grocery store in High Street successfully competed with these larger firms.

Boots, and other large retailers included the word 'cash' in their names to indicate that they only accepted cash payments.

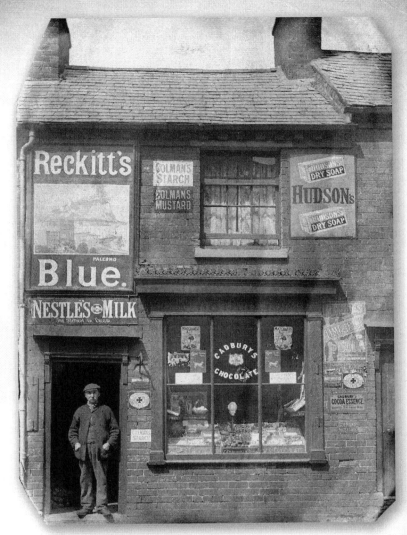

5. *Kidderminster shopkeeper, John 'Tiny' Watkins, standing in the doorway of his shop at 24 Hurcott Road. When he died in 1916 his widow, Emma, took over the shop. Their son, Jack, writing from France in late 1916 hoped she was 'doing good in the shop'. (Bob and Phill Millward)*

Those who could not afford to pay by cash could not take advantage of their reduced prices and for this reason, the chains tended to take the more affluent and reliable customers from the local shops, adding to their vulnerability.

The meat trade in Kidderminster demonstrates the state of retailing in 1914. Britain imported 40 per cent of its meat, some chilled but mostly frozen, and just under half was beef, mainly from South America. Independent butchers would not sell meat that had already been slaughtered and cut. F.G. Boswell, an independent butcher in Park Butts, advertised 'all home killed meat'. They bought their meat on the hoof, and slaughtered and cut it on their own premises. They relied on the Cattle Market, established in 1871 by Nock and Joseland, auctioneers, of Bank Buildings in Kidderminster. For example, a sale in 1916 included 821 separate lots, valued from 20s to £100 per lot, with 274 vendors and 225 purchasers of fat and store cattle, fat and store sheep, lambs, pigs and calves. Vendors came from a considerable distance, and when measures were taken to combat the spread of swine fever forty-nine pens were reserved for pigs from outside the scheduled counties of Gloucestershire, Worcestershire and Warwickshire.

Therefore, importers established their own chains of shops, where the meat was cheap but only cash was accepted. They flourished in textile towns like Kidderminster where extensive female employment meant families had enough cash to buy their products. On the eve of war they included Eastman's in Coventry Street, one of 1,400 shops, and the British & Argentine Meat Co. Ltd in the Bull Ring and Vicar Street. There was not the same hostility to the imports of cured bacon and hams, mainly from Denmark, which was leaner than home produced bacon. The meat was sold through specialist pork butchers, grocers and provision dealers, including the Danish Dairy Company in Worcester Street.

The threats from imports, and the damage to incomes caused by local price wars led independent butchers to band together to defend their trade, especially by setting local prices, and Percy Hanglin, who was to die at Katia in 1916 (see Chapter 4), was secretary of the Kidderminster and District Master Butchers' Association before the war.

There was one other bulk buyer that tradespeople feared – the Kidderminster Industrial Co-operative Society, founded in 1866. In 1912 there were four branches in the town, in Oxford Street, Worcester Street, the Horsefair, and Bewdley Road. One member of the original pioneer committee, Major Mills, was still a member of the board of management fifty years later, in February 1916, when the manager, George Allbut, organised a celebration for the sixty-five employees (6).

6. *A pub and small shops in the Horsefair, including a branch of the Co-op. On the left are: the Rifleman Public House (nearest the camera); Howell Brothers, bakers and Post Office; Mrs Alice Auty, milliner; Joseph Highfield, stationer (with awning); Mrs Ada K. Cartwright, hardware dealer (with awning); Henry Sprague, grocer, and James Ernest Monk, butcher (sharing); and Industrial Co-operative Society branch (with its name board angled forward). (Kidderminster Library)*

The Co-op sold food, clothing and household goods; it did not give credit, and it undercut the prices of the smaller shops. It paid a quarterly dividend to its regular customers or 'members' – a proportion of what they had spent – effectively undercutting their competitors still further. Small traders' hostility to the Co-op was still evident during the war years (see Chapter 5).

Not only was meat imported, but about 80 per cent of the grain consumed in Britain was also imported. Three millers in the town turned wheat into flour: D.W. Goodwin & Co. at the Town Mills in Mill Street; J.P. Harvey & Co. in Mill Street and Oxford Street; and Clement Dalley & Co. in Park Butts and the Horsefair. The town's numerous bakers produced the bread that was the staple food, in standard 4lb loaves – double the weight of the current 'large loaf'.

7. *Oxford Street,*
c. 1913, with the
Green Man and
Still on the left
describing itself as a
'Commercial Market
House'. On the right
is the Roebuck Hotel,
and in the distance the
Swan Hotel. The only
motorised transport
is the electric tram.
(Kidderminster Library)

Barley was mostly used to make the alcoholic drinks sold by the numerous public houses and beer retailers scattered throughout the town. There was one pub in the town for every 200–250 people. Many also served visitors to the town. The Green Man and Still in Oxford Street was a market house run by Miss Elizabeth Bytheway, who employed an ostler, Arthur Millman, to assist her with the fifty or more farmers' horses and carts that were put up in the yard on market days (7).

Wolverhampton & Dudley Breweries owned eighty of the town's pubs. The Angel Inn in Worcester Street and the Parkers Arms in Park Lane still did their own brewing, and there were four local brewers to supply the rest: Robert Allen & Co. in Orchard Street; Radcliffe & Co. at the Cross Brewery on Comberton Hill; the Kidderminster Brewery Co. in Blackwell Street; and Hopkins, Garlick & Co. at the Town Brewery in Mill Street.

On the eve of war, Kidderminster had a strong agricultural presence alongside its industry. There were about fifty farms, market gardens, nurseries, dairies, and cattle keepers encircling the town (Fact box 4). They included the Corporation Sewage Farm, of 760 acres, towards Stourport, which had a livestock of horses, one cow and calf, sheep and pigs. It was managed by George Stones for a salary of £200 p.a. together with a house, coal, lighting and transport, for which he was paid £26 in lieu of a horse. Some concerns were much smaller than this: Wilfred Weaver, market gardener of Stourbridge Road, worked 5 acres of land, kept pigs, had several hundred fruit trees and was also a greengrocer.

Dairymen and milk dealers often kept their own dairy cows, and Alice Wellings had been the proprietor of the Lark Hill Dairy for twelve years, helped by her son, Alfred, the cowman and stockman, and her daughter. They had twelve cows and nearly 40 acres. William Alfred Coates, dairyman, delivered 26 gallons of milk a day, while Howarth Brothers were milk contractors in Blackwell Street.

Coal was the main fuel for cooking and heating. Coal merchants and dealers in Kidderminster were concentrated in or near Station Yard, convenient for receiving their stock by rail. Some, in the vicinity of Clensmore, received their stock by canal. Others were in the town's suburbs near to their customers, who could collect the small quantities they wanted when they could afford them. Coal was also required for the railways and industry, both still powered by coal-fired steam engines.

Alternatives to coal were beginning to make an appearance, however, with the Gas Company in Pitts Lane enabling street lighting. The Kidderminster & District Electric Lighting & Traction Company generated electricity and operated the trams, whilst lighting in houses and workplaces was achieved by a variety of means – candle, oil, gas and electricity.

Fact box 4

AGRICULTURAL ACTIVITY IN KIDDERMINSTER

Number of farms, market gardens, nurseries, and dairy farms:

Stourbridge Rd	1
Wannerton	1
Hurcott	3
Birmingham Rd	1
Offmore	1
Comberton	7
Hoo Road	1
Reservoir Rd	1
Park Lane	1
Sutton	4
Bewdley Hill	1
Lea Bank Ave	1
Blakebrook	1
Habberley	6
Trimpley	9
Franche	9

Hospital provision had become very important. Kidderminster Infirmary and Children's Hospital in Mill Street, erected in 1870 at a cost of £10,700, was run by a management committee formed of the honorary medical staff and people elected by subscribers. The president, T.H. Charles, was a wealthy farmer at Park Attwood, and Albert D. Chambers, a practising chartered accountant, was the secretary and collector. On the eve of war there were three consulting surgeons – Samuel Stretton, Walter Moore and Edward Homfray Addenbrooke – and four other surgeons. These surgeons were all in private practice, from which they made their living, and gave their time and skills free to the infirmary. Some of them also held other medical posts in the town. E.H. Addenbrooke was medical officer of health to the rural district council, medical officer and public vaccinator for the Wolverley district of the Kidderminster Poor Law Union, and certifying factory surgeon. His son, Bertram, was also a surgeon captain in the local Territorial regiment. The honorary dental surgeon to the infirmary was Arthur L. Bostock, who had his own dental practice. Anne McFarlane, the matron, was the most senior person employed by the infirmary. It was a training hospital for nurses, and during the war nurses were trained for a month. Christine Tomkinson trained there between 11 August and 15 September 1915.

The main source of funding for the infirmary was the advance purchase of patient notes. Outpatient notes were 5s 3d, and inpatient notes cost one guinea (£1 1s). Before the war these bought two weeks' treatment at the hospital but, in February 1915, this was reduced to one week.

A bed reserved for a child from Hopton Wafers with tonsillitis cost one inpatient note. Groups of people raised money to buy them, and in 1915/16 Naylor's workers purchased eight inpatient and nine outpatient notes, while Lea's workers purchased three inpatient and eight outpatient notes for £5 5s. The parish churches of St Mary's, St Barnabus, Holy Trinity and St James pooled their collections to buy twenty-two inpatient and twenty-four outpatient notes. They could be used by any contributor who needed them.

The hospital served a wide geographical area, and Clee Hill Quarry Men's Union, Bewdley and Wribbenhall Mutual Help Society, Stourport Church Children's Service, and the parishioners of Elmbridge, Hopton Wafers and Doddington all purchased several notes. There were also many individual subscribers. In January 1916, Miss Pulley of Tunbridge Wells returned unused notes which the management proposed to 'give away to deserving cases'.

Another source of income for the infirmary, Saturday Collections among employees, was pioneered at Kidderminster. Established in the 1870s, the collections continued through the war. In 1915, among others, the employees of Victoria Carpets raised £10 10s, Woodward Grosvenor, £10, and Kidderminster Laundry, £1 1s. Those subscribing over £5 sent representatives to the Saturday Fund Committee which then nominated delegates to the management committee.

The doors of the infirmary were always open to accidents or emergencies. On 12 July 1916, Joseph Mole, aged 57 of Franchise Street, and employed at Naylor's, was sweeping waste from under a carding machine with a broom when a spike caught his elbow. He was taken to the infirmary, his elbow was bandaged and he was sent home. After two sleepless nights in pain, he returned to the infirmary and was kept in. The wound had been infected with tetanus (or 'lockjaw') and he eventually died. At the inquest, William Bird, described as a 'youth of Orchard Street' and 'hopper feed minder', explained that Mole was a card dresser who had been employed at the work for forty years. The man who usually pulled waste out with a rake was away ill and, therefore, Mole was doing the work himself. The verdict was accidental death.

As the bacillus causing tetanus lives in the soil injured soldiers were routinely given anti-tetanus injections from 1915 onwards, but it was not yet standard for non-combatants.

These institutions, large firms, small traders, and individuals would all play their part in the coming war (Profile 1).

THE THURSFIELD FAMILY

Thursfields family solicitors, was established in the 1870s. By 1914 Spencer Thursfield was in partnership with his eldest son, John Horace Thursfield, who was also town clerk.

John, a captain in the South Staffordshire Territorials, saw service at Hohenzollern where he won the Military Cross. In 1916, as lieutenant-colonel, he commanded his battalion on the Somme. Wounded, he returned to England. In 1917 he was wounded twice more at Cambrai and Passchendaele.

In his absence, Spencer Thursfield took over as town clerk, sat on the county appeal tribunal, the county council, and local fund-raising committees. His other children were also active in the war:

Raymond Spencer Thursfield, RN, was appointed paymaster commander to the 2nd Battle Squadron of the Grand Fleet. Honoured for his part in the Battle of Jutland, 31 May 1916, he received the Russian Order of St Anne in June 1917 and became a Companion of the Order of St Michael and St George in July 1919 for services as secretary to Vice Admiral Sir Arthur Leveson, commander of the Australian Navy.

Gerald Arthur Thursfield, senior chaplain to the Mesopotamia Expeditionary Force, saw fighting in Persia and was mentioned in despatches.

Aubrey Charles Thursfield commanded a torpedo boat and, later, fighting ships in Mesopotamia. He was also mentioned in despatches. He commanded HMS *Nymphe* in the Adriatic, for which he received a medal *'Pro Valore Militare'* from the King of Italy.

Lieutenant Henry Grosvenor Thursfield, commissioned into the Worcestershire Yeomanry in 1916, served in Egypt and Palestine and took part in the capture of Jerusalem and the freeing of Palestine.

Spencer's daughter, Margaret, was head cook at the Larches (Voluntary Aid Detachment) and later at other Red Cross hospitals.

Spencer's wife was active in the Sailors and Soldiers Families Association and other relief work, for which she received the thanks of Queen Alexandra.

The firm of Thursfields continues today.

(Mark Thursfield)

1

OUTBREAK OF WAR

On 28 June 1914 Franz Ferdinand, nephew and heir to Emperor Franz Joseph, was assassinated by Serbian nationalists in Sarajevo, Bosnia, part of the Austro-Hungarian Empire. This sparked a chain of events that was to lead to a world war.

Austria was predisposed to teach Serbia a lesson, however, recent wars in the Balkans and the arms race had made European powers highly sensitive to both real and imagined threats. Before acting, Austria sought assurance of support from Germany to counter any Russian support of the Serbs. Austria declared war on Serbia on 28 July and Russia, after gaining the approval of her ally, France, started preparing for war. Germany made a similar move, and sent ultimatums for Russia to suspend mobilisation and for France to declare its neutrality. However, the French feared a mobilised Germany, and on 1 August started its own mobilisation. Germany formally declared war on Russia, and the following day delivered an ultimatum to Belgium demanding the use of its territory in operations against France, and threatening to treat the country as an enemy if she resisted. On 3 August Germany declared war on France. On 4 August Britain sent an ultimatum to Germany to terminate military actions against Belgium. No offer of termination was received, therefore, at 11.00 p.m. Britain joined France and Russia at war with Germany.

On the day war was declared, the Worcestershire Regiment (Worcesters) (Fact box 5) had four regular battalions of full-time soldiers. Many of them were from Kidderminster, which had a strong tradition of military service. The 2nd and 3rd Battalions were mobilised immediately and landed in France on 14 and 16 August respectively. The 1st Battalion, which had been in Egypt, arrived back in England in October, and the 4th Battalion returned from Burma in February 1915. The 5th and 6th (reserve) Battalions, also full-time, were training battalions for home service only, sending drafts to the regulars and receiving recruits to replace them. They immediately went to their home defence war station at Plymouth, Devon.

The Worcesters' two Territorial battalions of part-time soldiers, the 7th, based at Kidderminster, and the 8th, based in Worcester, were at summer camp in Minehead, Somerset. After returning they set off for their war stations at the head of the Blackwater Estuary in Maldon, Essex, to defend against invasion from the North Sea. During the move, the men were invited to volunteer for service overseas and most did so, forming the 1/7th and 1/8th Battalions. The rest were withdrawn to form two new second line Territorial Battalions for home defence. The 2/7th Battalion returned to Kidderminster under the command of Colonel

Fact box 5

WORCESTERSHIRE REGIMENT

Existing battalions 1914:

Regular	1st – in Egypt (returned October 1914).	
	2nd – mobilised immediately.	
	3rd – mobilised immediately.	
	4th – in Burma (returned February 1915).	
Reserve	5th – mobilised immediately, home service only.	
	6th – mobilised immediately, home service only.	
Territorial	part-time soldiers intended for home service only.	
	7th and 8th battalions divided in September 1914.	
	1/7th – volunteered to serve abroad.	
	2/7th – did not volunteer to serve abroad.	
	1/8th – volunteered to serve abroad.	
	2/8th – did not volunteer to serve abroad.	

New battalions 1914–1918:

Territorial	3/7th	April 1915, depot/training.
	3/8th	April 1915, depot/training.
Service	9th	August 1914, K1.
	10th	September 1914, K2.
	11th	September 1914, K3.
Reserve	12th	November 1914, K4.
	13th	November 1914, K4.
Service	14th	September 1915, privately raised by H. Webb MP.
Transport workers	15th	December 1916.
	16th	March 1917.
Service	17th	May 1918, renamed battalion.
Garrison	1st (Reserve)	January 1916.

E.V.V. Wheeler and a campaign was launched to bring it up to strength. Recruiting staff were established at the Shrubbery, their drill hall, and the battalion was filled within three weeks.

Lord Kitchener, Secretary of State for War, realised that the army would require vastly increased manpower. Therefore, in August 1914, he appealed directly to the public for a new army of 100,000 men, hoping to add a battalion to each existing regiment, including a 9th battalion for the Worcesters. This was achieved in days, and was known as Kitchener's First Army (K1). By October, he had appealed for four more armies, K2, K3, K4 and K5, adding 10th, 11th, 12th and 13th battalions to the Worcesters.

Kidderminster men were not slow to respond to these calls to arms (8), they volunteered for the Territorials and Kitchener's Army, while others anxiously queried whether they were fit to enlist. Two other Territorial forces were based in the town: 'A' Squadron of the Worcestershire Yeomanry, and a battery of the Royal Field Artillery (RFA). Recruits were drilled at the

8. Military and civilian recruitment staff on the steps of the Town Hall in 1914. (Kidderminster Library)

Shrubbery and in the town's streets, and by late August 1914 it resembled a fortified town with so many men billeted in and around the area. Initially, the rate paid to householders for billeting a man was 3s 4½d per day but, in October 1914, this was reduced to 2s 3d per day, owing to the expected longevity of the billets.

Appeals for recruits were made in newspapers and on posters, and promoted in person by military personnel. A recruitment meeting of August 1914 was addressed by Colonel Hickman, who was touring Worcestershire. He claimed that Lord Kitchener had told him the county had done well but he hoped more could be achieved. Major Eric Knight, MP, explained that each man who enlisted would receive a soldier's pay, with a separation allowance for his wife of 1s 1d per day plus an extra 2d for each child. At a time when men were the main breadwinners, they needed to know that their families would not starve if they enlisted. Regulations stipulated that recruits must be 5ft 6in tall with a 35½in chest.

THE WAR.

Miss HARRISON

Will be pleased to Photograph ANY YOUNG MAN who is ABOUT TO JOIN THE ARMY, and send FINISHED PROOF FREE OF CHARGE (Order optional).

THE STUDIO, 36, STATION HILL.

9. Many recruits had their photographs taken in their new uniforms before going off to war. (Kidderminster Shuttle)

31

10. Young men transformed: portraits of Samuel Frederick Bell in civilian and military dress. He enlisted in the Royal Field Artillery in November 1915, aged 29.
(Nicky Griffiths)

Between 15 August and 12 September, over 320 men enlisted in Kidderminster and a fortnight later another 230 had been recruited. Miss Harrison, whose studio was on Station Hill, offered to photograph any young man about to join the army and send a proof free of charge (9)(10).

A major spur to recruitment was the Battle of Mons and the subsequent retreat. The small British Expeditionary Force of 70,000 men, battle-hardened in the wars of empire, including the 2nd and 3rd Worcesters, joined the French army in its resistance to the German execution of the Schlieffen Plan – a swift attack through Belgium, intended to knock France out of the war while the Russians were still mobilising.

A soldier from the 2nd Worcesters told how, on 22 August, 'by steady marching through the night [we] came to Mons where our entrenchments were made. On our left was what appeared to be a gas works and on our right the enemy'. The defensive position was behind the Mons-Condé Canal. The French, also to the right, were losing ground and suffering heavy casualties. They asked the British to hold their line for a day. Private Poulton from Spencer Street described how, on 23 August:

The Germans were sighted on the skyline – a distance of about 1,500 yards away. Our Maxims were at once brought to bear on them. The precision of our guns was wonderful – the Germans went down like nine-pins. They came on in a steady advance walking over their piles of dead. Our fire did great havoc – but so numerous were the enemy that it appeared to take no effect on their numbers.

Private Edmund Tandy of the Highland Light Infantry, a former member of Franche Football Club, gave another view:

They started shelling us … They had the range nicely, shells coming over like coconuts and I thought it was all over with me. Some of us started saying our prayers; others had forgotten them. It was like an inferno … There were thousands of them and our guns did fearful execution … but still they came on. We mowed them down with our rifle fire leaving them five and six deep … the shells whizzed overhead. One hit the gasworks and the noise was deafening. Whole houses were swept away.

The French decided to retreat, exposing the British to flank attacks and encirclement, forcing them to retreat as well. They were continually harassed, making a temporary stand at Le Cateau. The Germans were eventually halted 25 miles from Paris, after which they withdrew to a line they could hold.

A second stimulus to enlisting was the plight of Belgium and its people. Local men came away from Mons with both admiration and sympathy for the Belgian women, who brought refreshments to the marching soldiers, emptying their houses of food. Private Poulton recounted how 'the wife of the tobacconist stood at the door with an apron full of loose tobacco which she had emptied from jars and packets. We were invited to take a handful as we passed.' When the British had entrenched and were under fire, 'one Belgian woman made numerous journeys to her home close by and returned carrying bread to our men. Though she was in the firing line she persisted until a German bullet struck her in the head and killed her.'

Mary Anton, Suffragist and Fundraiser

Born in Scotland, Mary Ann Anton came to Kidderminster with her husband, George, when his firm, Victoria Carpets, transferred from Kirkcaldy in 1899. She was a member of the National Union of Women's Suffrage Societies, whose members – suffragists – were law-abiding campaigners for votes for women. In 1914, it transformed into the Active Service League to work for the war effort.

Within months Mary Anton was on the committees for the Prince of Wales Fund and the Belgian Refugees. She held an 'At Home' in 1915 at the Gables, in aid of hospitals for the wounded in Serbia and France, attended by 100 ladies. She frequently made donations to the infirmary and the Larches Red Cross hospital. She helped organise infirmary 'Pound Days'.

She was President of 'No 1 Household Association' for war savings. At a flag day, held to raise money for the Weavers' Superannuation Fund, she provided tea at the Corn Exchange and presented 100 straw baskets.

By 1916 she was the first woman member of the Board of Guardians. She was on the Food Economy Committee and took an active part in establishing the National Kitchen in 1918. She supported the temperance movement. After the war she was the first woman magistrate in Kidderminster. Her war work was recognised with an invitation to Buckingham Palace.

The photograph, taken early in the war, shows Mary Anton (left) with her four children: Isabella Winifred (back), born 1894 in Bonnyrigg, is probably Nurse Anton of the Larches Red Cross hospital; Charles Stewart (back), born in 1895 in Kirkcaldy, was a captain in the Royal Field Artillery, and was awarded the Military Cross, later he played cricket for Kidderminster; James Giles (front) was born in 1900 in Kirkcaldy; Mary's fourth child, Sheila Mary (next to her mother), was born in Kidderminster in 1909.

(Graeme Anton)

Therefore, when the first party of twenty-six Belgian refugees was brought to Kidderminster on 16 October 1914 everything possible was done for them. They were lodged in a four storey house in Church Street. The Gas Company supplied the gas and gas fittings free of charge and there was a collection of clothes, utensils, and other necessaries for them. By the end of the year, they had moved to the larger Spennells House. Kidderminster's Belgian Refugees Committee spent the afternoon of New Year's Eve with them, celebrating the passing of an unhappy year. Professor Baker's conjuring entertained them and this was followed by the lighting of the Christmas tree and the distribution of articles of clothing and general utility. Gifts for the refugee children were sent by Christmas ship *Jason* from the United States. Money continued to be raised for them with the Co-operative Women's Guild holding a whist drive, and a Belgian Easter Fete was held at the Town Hall and opened by Count van den Steen, Belgian minister at Luxembourg (Profile 2).

The result was an upsurge in volunteers for the armed forces. In Kidderminster, in the first few days of October, another

11. The war's high death rate was not expected. This advert appeared in the Kidderminster Shuttle *in October 1914. The offer was not available for long.*

400 men enlisted, and more Kidderminster men joined the Birmingham City Battalion (11).

By the end of 1914 British forces had suffered 90,000 casualties – killed, wounded and missing – larger than the entire force that had landed in August 1914, indicating the vast number of men needed to fight the war. Kitchener expected it to last at least three years. The government appealed for more recruits and letters to the local press encouraged anyone eligible to 'join at once'. The Motor Recruiting Scheme, set up in November 1914, collected volunteers by motor transport and took them by torchlight procession to a recruiting centre, accompanied by a band and Boy Scouts. It attracted fifty new recruits.

The Boy Scouts also had another job to do. There was a fear that enemy subjects were in Britain ready to attack key installations. In August 1914 the Scouts were put at the disposal of the chief constable and town authorities and urged to do whatever they could to help. They acted as messengers and guarded Hoobrook Viaduct, Bewdley Bridge, Lea Castle Bridge and the reservoir. Old Scouts were encouraged to assist, and young men not in the military were encouraged to join the organisation. They had to wear uniforms and carry their staves when on duty. They were, in effect, the first home defence force. The reservoir was still being guarded in 1916, when the mayor suggested that it was an unnecessary expense.

King Charles Grammar School started a cadet corps in 1914 under the command of Mr F. Telfer, given

---

Fact box 6

DEFENCE OF THE REALM ACT, 1914/15

Gave the government power to act to:

- Prevent communication with or assistance to the enemy.
- Secure the safety of the forces, ships, communications, railways, ports and harbours.
- Prevent the spread of false or malicious reports.

Gave the Admiralty or Army Council powers to:

- Require the output of any factory producing arms, ammunition or other warlike materials to be placed at its disposal.
- Take possession of any such factory and its plant for naval or military purposes.

[Added 16 March 1915:]

- Require the work in any factory to be done as they direct.
- Regulate work in any factory to increase production of war materials.
- Take possession of unoccupied premises for housing workmen or storage or transport of war material.

the rank of lieutenant. Early in 1915, it received the recognition of the War Office and by July it was part of a Worcestershire Cadet Battalion. The forty members marched in their new uniforms to join the rest of the battalion at Himley Park for ten days of exercises. Alongside these, a Civilian Rifle Association was formed to teach local non-combatants the art of rifle shooting, elementary drill and military training. It was a precursor of the Volunteer Training Corps, which eventually fulfilled 'home guard' duties (see Chapter 5).

The fighting forces needed munitions and other war materials (Fact box 6) and so skilled men were identified and exempted from military service. They were given 'On War Service' badges to wear, publicly declaring that they were 'doing their bit' for the war effort, and carried certificates (12) to protect them from being handed the white feathers which were used to accuse them of cowardice for not enlisting. The men who worked for Baldwin's, Hughes, Preston's, Prunell's and other munitions producers in Kidderminster were all badged (see Chapter 3).

Horses were another requirement of the enlarged army, needed for the mounted regiments and officers and for the transport of munitions and food at the front. A number of men

12. The badge certificate of Bernard French, electrical contractor at Pike Mills in Green Street. He was 29 years old in 1917. (Carpet Museum Trust)

NOT TRANSFERABLE.

This is to Certify that B French
employed by B French.
is authorised to wear War Service Badge
numbered J 26308 so long as he is employed
on work for war purposes by the employer
above named

Christopher Addison.

DATE OF ISSUE 22 JAN 1917   DATE OF EXPIRY   R.T.O.

in the county were authorised by the War Office to purchase horses on their behalf. The Castle Motor Co. quickly offered to help tradesmen who had lost their horses with deliveries, and then promoted its vans to fill the breach (13)(14).

However, not all sectors of the economy had such lucrative opportunities. Nationally, the carpet trade suffered badly in the first few weeks of the war. Production for August 1914 was down by more than a third compared with the previous year. In Kidderminster, carpet orders ceased and factories closed. During September orders began to trickle in, and the factories reopened, initially for three days a week, but there was still severe unemployment. Married men were re-employed first as they had wives and children to support. This gave unmarried men an additional motive for enlisting. K1, raised in August, had included a lot of unemployed men.

Carpet firms kept the jobs of their enlisted employees open against their return, and Tomkinson & Adam went further, paying their men maintenance allowances while they were in the forces, at a cost of over £1,000 per annum. A Relief Fund to help unemployed carpet workers was established in Kidderminster by Stanley Baldwin and Reginald Brinton. Jobs outside the carpet industry were sought for the unemployed, but carpet workers, particularly the women, were not necessarily suited to the manual labouring work available. However, the possibility of a large order for the carpet industry from the Admiralty gave some cause for optimism.

In December 1914, a consignment of 500,000 bags of flour was sent for the 'relief of the motherland' by the Canadian Government in response to the initial economic collapse. The Kidderminster Relief Fund was allocated 500 bags of this

13. *On 15 August 1914 the Castle Motor Company offered to help replace commandeered horses, for a price.* (Kidderminster Shuttle)

14. The Worcesters marching into the Bull Ring, c. 1914. The base of the Baxter statue is visible on the right. One of the horses, Punch, had been commandeered from Thomas Kench, cab proprietor in Lion Street. He became licensee of The Fox in Swan Street. (Carpet Museum Trust)

flour (about 70,000lb) and it was used regularly every week for about fifteen months. It was baked voluntarily by several bakers of the town and made about 15,000 loaves of 4lb weight, enabling around 230 loaves a week to be distributed to those struggling to survive.

At the declaration of war, the bank holiday was extended to prevent a run on the banks, and paper money was introduced (Fact box 7). Meanwhile, people started purchasing and hoarding large quantities of food, although this lasted no more than two weeks. C.W. Clarke, grocer in Coventry Street and Station Hill, informed the public that he had only supplied normal quantities to all his customers throughout August and did not regret that he had upset a few hoarders.

As the collapse of the carpet industry took effect, spending reduced and prices fell. B.L. Griffiths, grocer in Swan Street, having replenished his stocks after the hoarding, had decreased his prices (15), while Alexander Kerr & Co., tailors, were offering reduced prices in an effort to keep their staff employed.

The Panic rush for Food Stuffs

Having abated, and stocks being replenished, trade is becoming more settled, and some goods are

REDUCED IN PRICE.

B. L. GRIFFITHS, Grocer,
6, SWAN STREET, KIDDERMINSTER,

Is giving **GOOD VALUE, in face of high cost.**

Meanwhile, there was the first hint of things to come when a plea to Worcestershire women from Katherine Harley of Condover Hall, Shrewsbury, was published in September 1914:

> We cannot ask our men to recruit without offering them our help in carrying on the work they leave behind. Who amongst you will volunteer to take the place of a man in office, shop or factory, in order to release him for military service … I ask in the name of my brother who so sorely needs the service of the able-bodied men of our country.

Her brother was Sir John French, commanding the British Expeditionary Force in France.

As the initial waves of patriotism, shock and panic subsided, the pressure for more soldiers increased, meaning that even more men would leave the town, while its economy was about to move onto a full war footing.

15. *On 15 August 1914, B.L. Griffiths, grocer, hoped that the hoarding rush was over and offered price reductions. (Kidderminster Shuttle)*

41

2

GOING TO WAR

By 1915 the numbers of men enlisting were much reduced. It was estimated that no more than a third of the military age men in Worcestershire were in the armed forces (Fact box 8). Worryingly, about half of those volunteering were being rejected on medical grounds.

Recruitment campaigners redoubled their efforts – the minimum height was reduced to 5ft 1in, the chest measurement to 34in, and the weekly separation allowances were increased to 9s for the wife and 2s for each child. A recruiting office was opened in the Bull Ring, one of eighteen in the county. Adverts proclaimed, 'The Great Resolution for the New Year – I will be a man and enlist to-day!' (16). An advert for the Worcesters

16. *At least one tradesman catered for the pride of the newly enlisted soldiers.* (Kidderminster Shuttle)

informed that three battalions were now fighting for the honour of their country, adding, 'Be in time lads, before the door is closed.' The door was not going to be closed in a hurry.

Employers were also pressured. Adverts asked them four questions: had every fit man under their control been given the opportunity of enlisting; were the men's positions to be kept open; had they offered other help if the men would serve; were they still employing men who ought to enlist. Members of the Kidderminster Traders' Association adjusted their labour to release men who wanted to enlist.

Mr Greatwich had apparently done all he could to further recruiting, and his daughter held the gold medal for recruiting in the district. Dependents of borough policemen who volunteered were allowed 12s per week if married and 7s a week unmarried (half of the members had already volunteered). The fifteen Co-op employees who enlisted were allowed 5s a week.

Adverts for specific skills offered increased pay, increased age ranges or reduced the medical requirements. Saddlers and harness makers could be aged 19–45, wear glasses and earn 5s per day. Motor drivers, first class general smiths, electricians and steam lorry drivers would earn 42s per week. A special medical examination would ensure the acceptance of all men fit for motor driving. Blacksmiths and wheelwrights at 1s 8d per day, butchers and bakers up to the age of 40 and horse transport drivers aged 40–45 years were all wanted.

Men whose term of engagement had ended since the start of the war were encouraged to re-enlist. Volunteers who were rejected on

Fact box 8

ENLISTED MEN FROM WORCESTERSHIRE, FEBRUARY 1915

Serving at outbreak of war from Worcestershire:

Regular battalions (1st, 2nd, 3rd, 4th)	2,000 (approx.)
Special reserve battalions (5th, 6th)	1,300
Territorial units	3,200
Army Reservists	1,800
Subtotal	8,300
Enlisted between 4 Aug & 20 Jan	10,332
Total	18,632

Estimated total number of males in the county:

Between the ages of 19 & 38	56,222
Number of those who are serving	18,632
	(about 33%)

Parliamentary recruiting campaign:

Number who have come up for enlistment	1,124
Accepted (included above)	567
Number found medically unfit	557

WANTED

IMMEDIATELY

200 MEN

FOR

WORCESTERSHIRE

YEOMANRY

FOR SERVICE ABROAD.

Apply, personally or by letter, to

MAJOR ERIC KNIGHT, M.P.,

5147   **16, Silver Street, WORCESTER.**

17. *The town's MP was personally involved in recruiting for the Worcestershire Yeomanry, which he had once commanded.* (Kidderminster Shuttle)

medical grounds were invited to re-apply. No man who was organically sound would be refused. Home defence, garrison duty and administration could be performed by less fit men, releasing those fit for active service.

Major Knight, MP, personally appealed for 200 men willing to serve abroad to make up the numbers of the Worcestershire Yeomanry (17). This action was to weigh heavily on him a year later (see Chapter 4).

Another tactic, 'pals' battalions, worked best in larger centres of population like Birmingham. However, Kidderminster was a centre for enlistment and many local men served together. When Private J.W. Pagett, of 4th Worcesters, wrote home from Gallipoli he listed nine 'Kidderminster boys' in the battalion with him; he was one of four who had previously worked at Bradley and Turton's Foundry.

In September 1915, a poster displayed in Kidderminster read:

Soldiers on leave read this. If you want an extra day or two at home Captain Hutchinson at the Drill Hall will give you a day's extension for each recruit you bring in.

But there were now less than twenty new recruits a week, a long way from the heady days of 1914 when hundreds of men joined in a week.

People were certainly appreciative of those who did join the forces. In March 1915 local councillors conducted a house to house visit in St Mary's Ward to obtain the names of those serving in the forces for a Roll of Honour for the borough. They found that a total of 400 men were serving, or had served, in His Majesty's Forces during the war. Clensmore Street and Broad Street provided over sixty soldiers and sailors each, while Queen Street provided fifty-six. In Park Ward sixty-three men from Park Street were serving, forty-seven from Park Lane, forty-five from Wood Street, thirty from Chapel Street, and twenty from Spencer Street.

On the first anniversary of the outbreak of war the Mill Street Wesleyan Church produced a Roll of Honour of their members in the forces. Of the twenty-eight men listed, four had died.

Appreciation of the soldiers was also expressed by providing them with gifts or 'comforts'. By March 1915 a committee formed by Mrs Wheeler had sent 630 pairs of socks, 121 shirts, 241 vests, 1,024 mufflers, 1,178 pairs of mittens, 119 helmets, twelve handkerchiefs and nine pairs of gloves to soldiers in the Worcesters, at home and abroad. After March, mufflers and mittens were no longer required, but shirts and socks were needed throughout the summer. Gifts were collected by Miss Tomkinson via Tomkinson & Adam. Members of the National Women's Liberal Association made gifts for soldiers billeted in the town, holding Monday evening work meetings at the Girl Guides' rooms in High Street. By August, a Worcestershire Regimental Comforts Fund had been established in the county, collecting for both the infantry and

18. *A. Preedy & Sons, tobacconists in the Bull Ring, used a recent invention to advertise their wares.* (Kidderminster Shuttle)

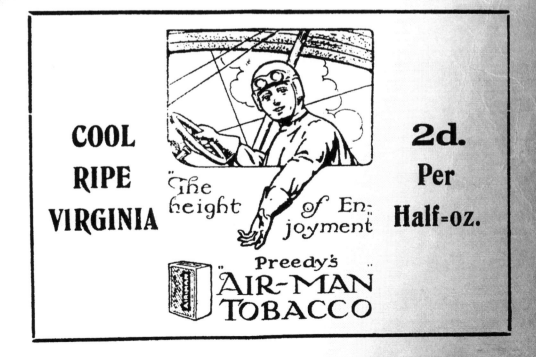

COOL RIPE VIRGINIA

"The height of Enjoyment

2d. Per Half=oz.

Preedy's "AIR-MAN TOBACCO

yeomanry regiments, while in December money was raised for Christmas puddings for the soldiers.

Individuals also sent gifts to their loved ones, and local shops stocked items the soldiers might appreciate. A. Preedy & Sons, tobacconists in the Bull Ring, informed customers that cigarettes could be sent to men in the Expeditionary Force at duty free prices by arrangement with the British and French Governments (18). Samuel Whitcomb, at the Knitting Depot in Wood Street sold specially prepared wool for knitting socks, mufflers, vests, and helmets for both army and navy.

Gifts were intended to be practical and helpful (19). They were much appreciated, and many letters of thanks were written. Walter Beddoes of Hurcott Road Bakery received a letter from Rifleman Darcy of the King's Liverpool Regiment thanking him 'for the kind present of the chocolates and cigarettes as they came in like pieces of gold. We had just come out of the trenches and feeling a bit dirty we were going into billets when one of my comrades, Crossley, got a parcel and gave the packets out. We opened our eyes in wonder.' Lance Corporal Graves, of 1st Battalion King's Own Royal Lancasters, wrote to the children of Foley Park School: 'Dear little Friends, – I have much pleasure in acknowledging the receipt of your gift of cigarettes, which we appreciate very much. We are all glad to know that our little school children think of those who are trying to do their best to end this terrible war. We trust peace is not far off.'

19. There were gifts for many aspects of trench life. (Kidderminster Shuttle)

Gifts were also sent back with soldiers returning from leave. Quartermaster Sergeant Harry Tranter of Stourbridge Road took a parcel of tobacco from customers at the Old Bear Inn for the men of his battery. The letter of thanks was signed by eight Kidderminster men.

In May 1915 Lord Kitchener appealed for another 300,000 men. Adverts asked people to, 'Remember Belgium and the *Lusitania*.' On 7 May 1915 a German U-boat torpedoed and sank the Cunard Liner *Lusitania*. One passenger who survived was Maitland Kempson, sales director at Woodward Grosvenor, returning from a business trip to the United States and Canada.

Amid increasing concern that the army would not be able to replace its losses, a letter from Lord Kitchener asked the mayor why more men were not coming forward. He replied that there was a perceived unfairness in the way some men went and some were exempt; more men would go if compelled by a law that was fair to everyone. Brinton already thought that conscription was necessary.

The National Registration Act of July 1915 was the first step in this direction. All persons between the ages of 15 and 65, male and female, were required to register, giving basic personal details, the name and address of their employer, their employer's business, whether they were working for a government department, and any other skills they possessed and were willing to use for work. In return they received a certificate of registration which they were to retain. The mayor, R.S. Brinton, organised the issue and collection of the registration forms. One collector was told, 'I shan't fill up no form. I wants to know first why the battalion have not gone to the front.' Not everyone appreciated the need for training or home defence.

Nationally, it revealed that, of 21.6 million names on the register, 5.1 million were men of military age with 1.5 million in reserved occupations. At least 3.4 million men technically able to join the forces had not yet volunteered. Lord Derby, Director of Recruiting, drew up a scheme requiring the voluntary attestation of all men between the ages of 18 and 40. Attestation was a legal undertaking to serve in the armed forces when called upon. Attested men wore army khaki or navy blue armbands. Local men who complied included Jack Watkins, carpet weaver, of

Longmore's Buildings in Hurcott Road (Profile 3) and **Reginald Sidney Amos**, a timekeeper temporarily living in Smethwick (20). But at the end of this exercise there were still 2 million men deemed available for military service who had failed to attest. The only solution was conscription.

The first Military Service Act of January 1916, operational from 10 February, provided for the enlistment of every unmarried male British subject, including widowers with no dependent children, aged over 18 and under 41 years. Exceptions were ministers of religion, men discharged from the forces through disablement or ill health, soldiers whose period of service had terminated, and those who had offered themselves for enlistment and been rejected. In May 1916, conscription was extended to married men. The other exceptions were also progressively withdrawn.

20. The attestation of Reginald Sidney Amos on 9 December 1915. Although a Kidderminster man, he had volunteered for war work and been sent to Smethwick to work at Sankey's who were making aircraft parts. (Ruby Henderson)

The Military Service Acts recognised a number of additional grounds for exemption from conscription: conscientious objection; work of national importance; exceptional financial, business or domestic obligations meaning serious hardship would ensue; and illness or infirmity. There was to be no exemption where the work could be undertaken by a woman or an older man.

A system of local tribunals was set up to receive, arbitrate and administer applications for exemption. In Kidderminster, a borough tribunal covered the town, and a rural tribunal covered rural Kidderminster and the surrounding villages. The borough tribunal was chaired by Reginald Brinton. The vice chairman was Alderman Michael Tomkinson, who also chaired the rural tribunal. Other members were leading businessmen and public servants of the town (Fact box 9). The clerk to the tribunal received applications, notified parties of dates of hearings, kept the register of decisions and, where appropriate, issued certificates of exemption. Both tribunals appointed advisory committees to make recommendations where the cases were uncontroversial and a hearing unnecessary.

The tribunals were courts of law. The parties to a case were the applicant arguing for exemption, who could choose to be represented by a lawyer (often H.G. Ivens, a solicitor in High Street), and the military representative, usually a retired officer, arguing for conscription. Cases were heard in open court with the press present, but individual applicants could request private hearings. The tribunal members were the judges. If they decided to grant an exemption it could be absolute, conditional or temporary, or cover combatant service only. Most of the exemptions granted in Kidderminster were temporary, usually for three or four months, entailing repeated applications to the tribunal for further exemptions. Each successful applicant was issued with a certificate giving the terms of their exemption (21).

If either party was dissatisfied with the decision they could resort to the appeal tribunal, based in Worcester and chaired by J.W. Willis Bund, who said that local tribunals had to 'take the greatest possible care that there was no undue interference with the liberty of the subject, and to see that everything was done in a fair and most impartial manner.'

JACK WATKINS' FAMILY PHOTOGRAPH

Jack Watkins, of Hurcott Road, was a weaver at Victoria Carpets. Having attested in December he was called up in June 1916. He was photographed with his family: sons Cyril and Bill (front), wife Ruth, daughters Phyllis, Clarice and Ruth (front).

His last letter home mentions them all:

I hope Willie got his Birthday Card in time for I shall be thinking of him on the 21st ... I hope Cyril got the watch that I sent him for I know it would please him better than anything, he will want me to keep soldiering if I keep sending him presents, but I hope he will be a good boy and do what you tell him. I also hope Clarice is a good girl and hope she will help you and her granny while I am out here. I hope Ruthey & Willie & Phyllis are all going on well. ... from your ever loving Husband & Dad.

On 16 February 1917 the 2nd Worcesters, including Jack, moved into the front line at Clery sur Somme. The following day Jack was killed by shell fire. Lance Corporal John Smith wrote to Ruth, '... we had struck up a good friendship ... More than once he told me things about his private life & showed me the photo of yourselves & the children ...'

Ruth was upset that Jack had volunteered, leaving his family in the lurch, and had to be persuaded to submit his name for the war memorial. Nevertheless, she kept his documents safe, and a large framed version of the photograph hung in her living room.

Ruth's grandson, Phill, visited and photographed Jack's grave in Peronne. Ruth was so grateful that she gave him the collection of documents.

(Bob and Phill Millward)

The ultimate appeal was to the central tribunal in London. No applicant was enlisted until their case had been decided, including appeals. However once a man was called up, the jurisdiction of the tribunal ceased.

There were a number of local military representatives, although, by law, only one was involved in each case. The most senior was Colonel the Honourable Reginald Henry Bertie (1856–1950) of Rycote House, Oxfordshire, and a younger brother of the Earl of Abingdon. He had commanded the 2nd Battalion Royal Welsh Fusiliers. Whenever he attended the tribunal in Kidderminster he had lunch with the Tomkinsons. Another representative was Major Ellis William Talbot, a solicitor in Church Street, who served in the Territorials for many years after joining in 1875. He dealt with a number of cases heard by the tribunal and was consistently present at the Advisory Committee meetings. A third, J.T. Pilling, was not a local man, possibly coming from a Lancashire family. He moved to Wolverley Court, no more than a couple of miles from Kidderminster, in about July 1916. Thereafter, he was the main military representative at Kidderminster's borough and rural tribunals.

Although tribunal papers were destroyed after the war on the orders of the government, as they contained personal information, the borough tribunal register of decisions still survives and includes minutes of key administrative items. The hearings were also extensively reported in the local paper, which gave valuable pertinent and incidental information for many cases.

A number of cases show the extent and limitations of the tribunal's powers. One of the earliest cases heard by the tribunal was brought by Mrs Smallman of Dudley Street, who wanted exemption for her son who had joined the navy; but the tribunal could not take any action because he had already enlisted. George Jones of Habberley Road, was a groom and gardener for the Misses Goodwin. This was non-essential work so, when Major Talbot 'claimed' him for the army, his application for exemption was 'not assented to'. Another, Cyril Gray, was a clerk at George Law's who had been given a temporary exemption to allow him to finish supervising a government contract. In late February 1916 he informed the tribunal that the work was nearly finished and he did not request any further extension. Alderman Tomkinson commented, 'That is the spirit we like to see'. Clarence Penson, brewer's clerk of Chester Road, showed similar spirit. He had attested with the 'most earnest desire to render military service' but since then his wife had become seriously ill.

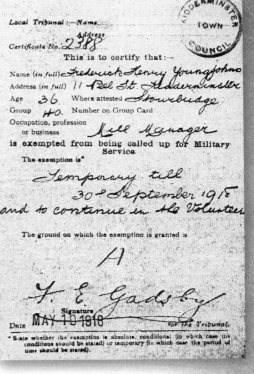

21. *The certificate of exemption of F.H. Youngjohns, aged 36, foreman in the Turkey Department at E. Hughes & Son. He superintended a patented loom with which no one else was familiar. (Carpet Museum Trust)*

The general perception that single young men should be the first to fight for their country was evident when conscription was extended to married men, and the Advisory Committee, chaired by Councillor Frederick Tandy, a beer retailer in Wood Street, immediately recommended that married men be given temporary exemptions *en bloc*, to delay their call-up. Colonel Bertie regarded this as 'most irregular' but there is no evidence that it was rescinded.

Attempts were made to manipulate the tribunals in order to obtain exemption. One way was to attend tribunals at other centres. Applicants were usually granted leave to appeal against the tribunal's decisions, if requested, but H.W. Snape of Chester Road, who had already been refused exemption by the Bewdley and Worcester appeal tribunals, had leave to appeal again refused.

There was a concern that men had recently entered some occupations specifically in order to escape military service. Applicants were told to bring their registration cards to their hearings because, as was observed, 'some are not in the occupations they were when they were registered. They thought they would be safer in some other occupation.' Anonymous letters alleged that certain men had lied to the tribunal, but the letters were 'not read'. The recruiting officer in Stourbridge also received some about men not joining the army and observed that it was 'worthless to worry him with such letters concerning such men, as not a single recruit had been obtained by such letters.'

Where cases were perceived as genuine the tribunal could show considerable sympathy. William R. Taylor, an under-foreman at Brinton's, who lived in Franchise Street, had two brothers serving in the forces, another brother had died and his father had been unable to work for several years, so he was the sole support of the household. This was regarded as a hard case and he was given temporary exemptions.

The best known applicants for exemption were conscientious objectors, although they were only a tiny proportion of the total number. Austin Cauldfield, shoemaker in George Street, appeared before the tribunal in March 1916. He claimed that his conscience and religion prompted him to

---

Fact box 10

ARGUMENT AGAINST AUSTIN CAULDFIELD, CONSCIENTIOUS OBJECTOR

Mr Field: 'You say you are a conscientious objector. Do you believe in the Bible?'

Applicant: 'Yes. I daresay certain texts contradict one another.'

Mr Field: 'You believe in the doctrine of the Bible?'

Applicant: 'Certainly.'

Mr Field: 'It teaches you to fight the devil.'

Applicant: 'Yes, and to refrain from evil.'

Mr Field: 'Where is there a bigger devil than the Kaiser? Do not you think you ought to fight him?'

Applicant: 'Perhaps he is. I have a conscientious objection to fighting.'

Mr Tomkinson: 'Are you a Christadelphian?'

Applicant: 'I am a Roman Catholic.'

In reply to Mr Porter, applicant said he should not object to working at his trade in the army. He would work in a hospital.

Mr Field: 'But not assist in fighting the devil?'

Applicant: 'It is man's duty to bring life into the world, and, when he has brought it in, to preserve it.'

refrain from taking life in civil life, and in warfare if he took life he was guilty of murder, and no government or tribunal had the power of taking that guilt away. His interrogation was published verbatim, because the tribunal's argument against conscientious objection was regarded as particularly strong (Fact box 10). His plea was dismissed. He appealed, but withdrew it in May, having 'been converted', and enlisted. He married in September, by which time he was a driver in the Army Service Corps. It is tempting to wonder if it was his future wife who persuaded him to enlist.

S.E. Hughes, a locomotive fireman, was a Christadelphian, a sect which had publicly proclaimed its conscientious objection to military service over several decades. He was recommended for non-combatant service, but was exempt as long as he remained with the Great Western Railway Co.

G.R. Lambert, a conscientious objector due to appear before the appeal tribunal when it sat at Kidderminster, though not necessarily from the town, was unable to attend because he had been arrested and was held in gaol. The tribunal ruled that he was an Englishman, and should therefore be heard. He attended a month later escorted by an officer from Winson Green Prison. He said he was willing to do agricultural work, and the chairman, observing that it was recognised as work of national importance for conscientious objectors, ordered him to find such work within twenty-one days. Lambert gratefully thanked the court for the order.

All men applying for exemption had to have their fitness assessed by the Recruiting Medical Board in Worcester before their case was heard. When Frank Coates, a hairdresser of Blackwell Street, asked for absolute exemption on grounds of 'organic unsoundness' due to a valvular disease of the heart, the doctors' certificates that he submitted were contradictory, and led the chairman to exclaim 'These doctors!' That month, September 1916, a Special Medical Board had been set up in London to re-examine men who were passed fit by a Recruiting Medical Board but who had produced doctors' certificates stating that they had long-term illnesses or were otherwise unfit. The tribunal sent Coates to London to be examined.

In September 1916 a letter from the War Office, read out at the rural tribunal, referred to the large number of less fit men among the recruits, and stated that it was general service men they wanted and the services of the less fit were not so urgently required. However, with the heavy losses of men on the Somme from July 1916 (see Chapter 4), they quickly discovered that they needed men of almost any fitness. Many Kidderminster men who had been placed in a low fitness category were now deemed fit enough to be called up.

Several complained about the quality of the medical examination and often the tribunal was sympathetic. W. Taylor, aged 36, a coal dealer and sweep in Woodfield Street, claimed that his hearing was defective, but the doctor had not even examined his ear. Pilling responded that his deafness might be an advantage as he would not hear the big guns so badly. However, he was eventually exempted. Harry Bunn, aged 42, a painter, suffered from rheumatism, but the doctor had only looked at him and told him to get back to his painting as he was no good for the army. The tribunal observed that medical examinations were very confusing. Harold Hunt, aged 33, a cooper of Wood Street, claimed that he was 'literally a walking hospital' as he had undergone several operations. He was exempted.

Matters came to a head at the rural tribunal in September 1918. The tribunal, and Pilling, had written to the Worcester recruitment office on behalf of one particular man, but their letters had been ignored and he was called up. Within a month he was back home with a new suit and a pension of 20s a week. According to Alderman Tomkinson, the medical examination at Worcester had been an absolute scandal. It was felt that unfit men were being called up by the authorities without regard to the opinion of local tribunals who personally knew the men and their capabilities. Tomkinson looked through the list that day and found that out of 102 men before them only six were in the top fitness category.

Enlistment in the peacetime army was for a specific length of time. For some soldiers this expired during the war, and most lengthened their service to the end of the war, a date and time then unknown, having a month's leave before re-joining their battalion.

But some had seen enough of the fighting front, and chose not to re-enlist. By late 1916 they were eligible for conscripting back into the army and some came before the tribunal: J. Whitemore, aged 31, of Sutton Road, a fully fit bus driver for the Tramway Company, claimed that he had already 'done his bit' for the country. A year later, he was assessed at a lower level of fitness, and disingenuously claimed that if his health had remained good he would still have been in the army. By then he was a driver for J.H. Round of the Lion Hotel and exemption was refused.

Men who had been invalided home from the fighting were also eligible for conscription, providing their health had recovered sufficiently. Albert Oliver, who had worked for Naylor's for many years, was being called up again after a year less one day with the forces at the front. Major Talbot said, 'It shows how dreadfully short the army is of men. I am sorry to say it but I think I must claim him for the army.' Oliver referred to the number of single young men 'knocking about town', which prompted Mr Porter to respond, 'The only difference is this: one lot are getting a bit and the others are doing their bit.' Oliver was given an exemption. Vincent J. Hill, aged 32 of Broad Street, was a fully fit builder's labourer who had been at the front for a considerable period. He had three wounded stripes on his sleeve. He asked to be re-examined but was given an exemption.

The shortage of men led the government to broaden the recruitment criteria. Therefore, by late 1918, many of the applicants before the tribunal were aged 41 or over. J. Carss, of Bewdley Street, headmaster of Foley Park School, pointed out that there were only four male teachers left in the borough and how important it was to keep teachers in schools; they were doing jobs of national importance. He was exempted.

On 25 April 1917, a letter from the military authorities called attention to the need for a further 500,000 men for the army by 31 July next. The Battle of Arras was underway, and the Battle of Passchendaele would start at the end of July, both involving heavy loss of life (see Chapter 4). The pressure for more men to replace those lost in the war led to increasing criticism of any exemption from military service. The government, the military, the tribunal and the public were to blame each other for any shortfall. The tribunal implied that the military were not doing their job properly, by asking if they were satisfied that the men protected by certificates were in full work. In January 1918 the tribunal informed the Ministry of National Service, established a year earlier to oversee conscription, that 'a man named "W.R. Wilson" who had been twice not assented to by the local tribunal and appeal tribunal was still in civil life and ask for an explanation.' This was William R. Wilson, of Linden Avenue, assistant superintendent of the Prudential Assurance Company. He was quickly called up.

In late June 1918, the Ministry of National Service set about strengthening conscription and clarifying the role of tribunals. A decision of the central appeal tribunal relating to the last surviving son of a widow may have influenced the case of Horace Moule, aged 17, who applied on the grounds that three of his brothers had been killed in the war. The tribunal wrote to the War Office asking that he be put in a non-combatant corps. Gadsby later reported that 'the letter had had the desired effect'.

Specialist tribunals and commissioners were appointed to deal with some occupations. A war munitions tribunal had existed since 1915; a fuel overseer dealt with applications from men in the coal and fuel trade; the County War Agricultural Committee dealt with agricultural matters; and the Divisional Food Commissioner and the Regional Director for Livestock Commissioner dealt with appropriate applications.

This improved organisation took the antagonism out of the tribunal's dealings with those in authority. However, there was still hostility from the public. In October 1918, A. S. Perrett of Yew Tree Road wrote 'protesting against Mr Field remaining a member of the tribunal and sending men to the army whilst he himself came out on strike with the railwaymen.' No reaction or response to this letter was recorded.

Many conscripts were, in fact, willing to serve. At a meeting of the Kidderminster Chamber of Commerce the secretary, Spencer Thursfield, announced that Mr Sparry, who took the minutes, had been called up and would join the forces at once, not attending another meeting until after the war. He was wished good luck and a safe return. Conscripts were now sent where they were most needed, and Kidderminster men were no longer concentrated in the Worcestershire forces.

Men from all walks of life in Kidderminster joined the forces, especially from the carpet industry (Fact box 11). Unfortunately, the figures do not differentiate between volunteers and conscripts. Men from other parts of the local economy also enlisted. C. Dalley & Co., seed merchants, had lost twenty men by April 1916, and another sixteen had attested. F.G. Samman, of 6 Oxford Street, was fortunate to find someone to take over his business, but this was not always practical (22). Many other men from Kidderminster also joined the forces. The number of students at the School of Art and Science had reduced from 600 before the war to 500 in 1916. The 100 students from Dudley Training College who joined the army, included many from the town. Private A. Brimfield, a Kidderminster man, of the King's Light Infantry, had returned from Australia to enlist.

The large families of the time could have several sons in the forces. Six sons and a son-in-law of the Harper family of Mill Lane were in the forces. They had all been in service as grooms, coachmen or chauffeurs before the war, which was reflected in their army occupations. Albert was in the Army Remount Service, William was a gunner with the Royal Field Artillery, Alfred was in the Army Veterinary Corps, Walter was with the Midland Field Ambulance, Frank was in the Mechanical Transport Motor Ambulance Section of the Army Service Corps, Leonard was with the Motor Transport Army Service Corps, and Frederick Tilt was in training with the Worcestershire Yeomanry.

Fact box 11

ENLISTMENTS FROM THE CARPET INDUSTRY

Tomkinson & Adam	93	by July 1915
	171	by end of war.
Naylors	25	by February 1916.
Greatwich	52	by June 1916.
Victoria Carpets	64	by 1917.
Empire Carpet Works	45	by July 1917.
Woodward Grosvenor	82	by April 1917.
Carpet Manufacturing Co.	255	by July 1917.

Numbers enlisting from other carpet firms were probably similar.

22. In August 1915, F.G. Samman left his business in the hands of a manager and enlisted. After the war, Nicholls had his own tailor's business in Shrubbery Street. (Kidderminster Shuttle)

J. Mallard of East Street, a weaver at Woodward Grosvenor, had five sons, all married, serving in the forces: John, previously a tram driver in Birmingham, had been in the army for five months with the Royal Engineers; Arthur, painter for Mitchells & Butlers in Birmingham, was in the Coldstream Guards; Frank had already served in South Africa and Samoa, and had been working in a munition works in Birmingham before re-enlisting with the Worcesters; Percy had enlisted with the Yorkshires in September 1914, leaving a job with Woodward Grosvenor; and William, a sergeant in the regular army, went out with the first Expeditionary Force and was invalided home after seven months in the trenches.

The rapidly expanding army needed numerous additional officers (Fact box 12). Those in the reserve and recently retired were recommissioned, small numbers of officers were taken from Regular battalions, and temporary commissions were granted to suitable men, especially those in Officers' Training Corps at the universities, Inns of Court, public and grammar schools. Several men in Kidderminster, often sons of its more prominent inhabitants, were commissioned as officers. Three became lieutenants in August 1915: Ronald Adam, of Tomkinson & Adam; Geoffrey S. Tomkinson, son of Alderman Tomkinson; and Ronald A.W. Painter of Cobden Street, who was managing clerk to Talbot's solicitors in Church Street.

As the war tore families apart, taking the recruits away from all home comforts, letters assumed critical importance. From home they were addressed by giving the soldier's rank and name, his battalion or fighting unit, and the force he was in (23). Post Office staff were entrusted with top secret knowledge of the deployment of British forces so that the mailbags could be sent to the right part of the front. When they reached France they became the responsibility of Royal Engineers (Postal Section) to take to Brigade Headquarters. From there, mail went to the regimental post orderlies who collected it by horse and cart. Letters were handed to the men with their evening meal, usually on the second day after posting. There was a similar arrangement for the Royal Navy, with letters being sent to appropriate British ports for distribution offshore by the Admiralty Mail Officers.

The soldiers' letters home were collected and did the same journey in reverse. G.T. Cheshire & Sons, stationers in Vicar Street, sold army and navy writing kits for the men at the front, including writing paper and pencil, in a strong envelope ready for posting at 6½d.

Attempts were made to ensure that every soldier was able to correspond with someone at home, even if he had no family. Vera Brown, daughter of the stonemason Archibald Brown of Coventry Street, was a schoolgirl who corresponded with a soldier in France. She was not allowed to know his name, but he obviously appreciated her letters. He sent her and her mother, Helen, some of the souvenir embroidered postcards that were produced in France (24).

Fact box 12

A BATTALION, ITS SUBDIVISIONS AND ITS OFFICERS

Battalion (1,024 men)
  Commanded by lieutenant colonel.
  Second in command, senior major.
  Adjutant.
  Quartermaster.

Battalion headquarters
  Signallers.
  Transport.
  Machine guns.
  Band and drums.

A battalion is divided into four companies:
  Each company commanded by major or captain.

A company is divided into four platoons:
  Each platoon commanded by lieutenant or 2nd lieutenant with a sergeant.

A platoon is divided into four sections:
  Each section commanded by an NCO, i.e. corporal or sergeant.
  twelve men.

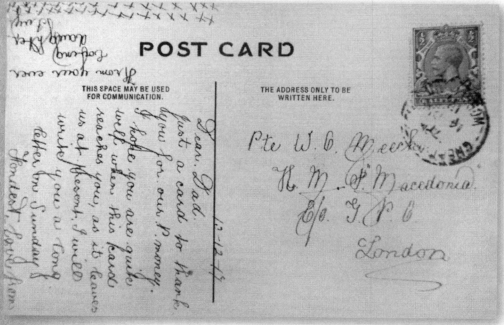

23. *This postcard of Kidderminster Railway Station, sent to Private W.O. Meech by his 13-year-old daughter, shows the minimal address required. Meech had served in both the Merchant Navy and Royal Navy before settling with his wife and three children in Wellesbourne Hastings, Warwickshire, in 1910/11. (Carpet Museum Trust)*

24. *A postcard sent to Vera Brown by her anonymous soldier correspondent. (Catherine and Peggy Guest)*

Shortages of recruits did not mean immediate front line service. Whether volunteers or conscripts, they needed to be trained. It was only in April 1915, after eight months vigorous training, mainly in Cheltenham, that the 11th Worcesters, part of Kitchener's third army, were fully equipped and ready for active service. However, the battalion, which included at least twenty-one Kidderminster men, did not cross to France for another five months.

As recruits poured in at the start of the war, army facilities quickly proved insufficient. Men had to remain at home, or in makeshift billets, drilling locally until more camps could be constructed, with wooden huts or tents to house them. H.L. Thompson, builder of Bridge Street, may have been one of those hurriedly making the huts. He was badged for building sheds for government contracts.

The training camps could be enormous. In August 1916 it was reported that W.H. Horton, previously a carpet designer at Morton's, was in training 'at a fine camp of huts' with about 60,000 men who were all looking fit (25). Letters from the new Kidderminster recruits told of the rigours of training:

> We were so busy we didn't know what day it was … Sunday was a welcome rest after 16 miles in full kit. Usually it was an hour's physical drill every day before breakfast, followed by a route march and then military drill. It's making us hard as nails … [There's] plenty of food and good money even if we do need to work 16 hours a day. A number of first recruits had a rough time with blistered feet – but they kept on smiling. We have a decent billet, some of us in a barn, however there was plenty of straw so it wasn't so bad even if there was an accompaniment of rats.

For one man it was too much: Wilfred Edward Bullen, aged 28, a boot repairer of Bromsgrove Street and secretary of the Boot Traders Association, joined 2/7th Worcesters in June 1915. Complications arose from bad colds he had contracted due to camp life and he died in January 1916 without ever seeing the front line, as the battalion was only ordered abroad in May 1916.

The officers of the 2/7th Worcesters gave their men a pipe and 1oz of tobacco each as a Christmas gift in 1914. As they were still billeted locally, most were able to spend Christmas with their families. However, by then the artillery were in a camp at Inglestone Common, Gloucestershire, where their leave was stopped on Christmas Eve with no rations provided, and they spent the holiday in up to 3ft of mud and slept in barns and stables. The Yeomanry were in King's Lynn, Norfolk, and were called back just two hours into their journey home for Christmas, although Lord Dudley and the other officers provided them with a Christmas lunch of roast beef, turkey and plum pudding. These sudden decisions to stop Christmas leave may relate to the unofficial Christmas truces that took place on the front line that year, when the soldiers of both sides met in the middle of no-man's-land, exchanged gifts, sang carols or played football matches. The nephew of Charles Dunn, draper, of Worcester Street, wrote, 'Singing and talking was heard. Our men greeted the enemy with a handshake and a gift of cigarettes and perhaps a tin of bully beef.'

In January 1915 the 2/7th Worcesters, about 1,000 men, marched to Lea Castle Park, Wolverley, where they were inspected by the Marquis of Salisbury. The following month a training camp in Northampton was ready to receive them, after nearly four months' training in Kidderminster. They departed in two trains from the railway station, where large numbers of people came to see them off and wish them good luck. A letter from Colonel E.V.V. Wheeler, their commander, was published in the *Shuttle* expressing:

> My thanks for the kindness shown to us during our stay here. Everyone, whether in our official or private capacity, has seemed anxious to assist us in every way.
>
> I should also like to thank those who have so liberally responded to the appeal made for comforts for my men. The good feeling shown towards us by everyone has helped to make our work easier and our stay in Kidderminster a time upon which we can look back with pleasure.

The recruits of 1914/15 formed part of an expanded army that took over an increasing proportion of the Western Front, but they were not ready for combat until the winter of 1915/16. As it was not practical to launch a winter offensive in the sodden landscape of northern France, which needed time to dry out, the summer of 1916 was the first opportunity to use this expanded army.

After the months of training the journey to the front was a time of both excitement and nervousness. In August and September 1915, Lewis Clifford Bratt used a pocket book to keep brief notes of the experience. He had his 25th birthday while on the journey. His home was in George Street, where his father had established a carpentry business. Lewis and his fellow soldiers set out from Bordon in Hampshire on 27 August 1915, arriving at a rest camp outside Le Havre the next day. Lewis wrote letters to his sweetheart, Nell, and his mother, and sent postcards to his brothers, Stan and Claud. On 29 August they boarded a train to St Omer. The journey took eighteen hours, and he slept on a stool in a cattle truck accompanied by the terrible rattle. They arrived at St Omer at 9.00 a.m. the next day, unloaded the wagons and started marching to their camp. They had eaten nothing since the previous evening and were very hungry. At 12.30 they were given two biscuits and a small amount of cheese:

> Kept on marching, all of us dead beat now. Marched about 14 miles to our billets. Got to billets had to go on guard all night with no rest till 6.30 next morning … Nothing to eat all night or drink. Paraded at 10.30, nearly up. Got into straw no blankets & slept till about 5.30. Very fine now, no effects of march, feeling tip top.

His fitness enabled him to deal with such exceptional demands.

They stayed at the billet at 'Bertehem', (possibly Boesegham) 10 miles south-east of St Omer, for the next five days. On Monday, 6 September, they started a two day trek, of about 20 miles each day. He got a sore throat and cold, and slept overnight in a very cold brick kiln. 'All men dead beat, all of us very footsore. All stone sets, insteps swelling.' They eventually reached a camp outside 'Baillieux' (probably Bailleul), about 15 miles from Boesegham on the map. Lewis had a good night's sleep in a barn that the Germans had used for a hospital, and felt a lot better the next day. It was a rest day and his birthday. He received a letter, birthday card and parcel from his mother and another parcel from 'dear Nell'.

They were now able to hear the big guns at the front. The next few days were spent cutting brushwood and trees, making hurdles for the trenches, sharpening the tools and moving billet once again. He noted: 'Passed farm where Germans shot fifty men & saw bullet holes in windows etc.' He was also making a bracelet for Nell, and had time to receive letters from home and a tobacco parcel from his mother, and to write more letters himself.

On 12 September, they started trekking at about 4.00 a.m., passing through Estaires, and reaching a billet 2 miles from the firing line:

Can see shrapnel shells bursting & aeroplanes & firing artillery quite close about 600 yards or so from where I am sitting. Makes you jump a bit. Saw a lot of ruins on way & damaged churches. … saw fine duel in air this morning, German brought down – grand. … Had eggs & chips for supper tonight, fine feed, 4 eggs & two lots of chips.

26. The pocket book of Lewis Clifford Bratt. This page shows a gap of a month while he was in hospital, and records his sending of 'the letter' to 'Nell', almost certainly a proposal of marriage. (Andra Kleanthous)

He bought a postcard for Nell sending 'Hope & Love', and tobacco and cigarettes were issued. Food and tobacco rations improved as the men got nearer the front. They were being slowly acclimatised to the war zone and this continued as they moved forward to the trenches, though it did not help everyone. On 14 September they moved billet to 'Amaintain' (either Armentieres or a place in the vicinity). Lewis 'had a walk round in afternoon. I got a bit of shrapnel from a house shutter. All ruined houses here. Piece of shrapnel hit one of mates in back, cut his coat & grazed his shoulder. A bit hot here.'

That night they went into the trenches for the first time, coming out very early the next morning. However, 'my pal Fred King was shot this morning through the head'. After a rest during the day they returned to the trenches that night, when the 'Germans set fire to farm in our lines. Snipers still very busy, altered road home because of snipers.'

They moved billets and went into the trenches again at night where, 'another of Company shot in ribs tonight.' The next day, Sunday 19 September, they went into the trenches for the first time during daylight, when Lewis was able to see the German trenches. As the danger increased, contacts with home became more important and the letter writing had not stopped: 'Had letter & Woodbines & Paper [probably writing paper] from Dearest Nell, cake & Woodbines from Claud. Wrote to Darling Nell tonight in Green envelope.' On Monday 27 September they shifted billets again.

The next entry was a month later on 29 October and records, 'came out of hospital …' He did not recount how he came to be there (26)(27).

27. 'Nell' (Ellen Bennett) accepted the proposal of Lewis Bratt, as this wedding photo of 1916 shows. (Andra Kleanthous)

3

WORK OF WAR

During the first twelve months of the war carpet production fell by 45 per cent due to shortages of labour, materials and orders. Labour was an obvious problem, with many workers enlisting. Tomkinson & Adam were unable to replace more than half of their enlisted employees, leaving looms standing idle, as work in munitions factories was more lucrative. By July 1915 their workforce had fallen by 260, and in July 1918 there were just 751 employees, little more than half the pre-war number. They employed women on men's work, but never more than twenty-five, and even then they could not get enough female employees. (28).

In April 1916, the government removed the carpet industry from the list of Certified Exempt Trades. At the same time, some attempt was made to ease the shortage of labour. The government issued a general order allowing women and young persons to work up to six hours overtime a week where the work done on behalf of the Crown and for export exceeded 75 per cent of their output. In June the order was extended until early August because of urgent government requirements, almost certainly in preparation for the Somme offensive. Greatwich was so far engaged on government work that the Home Office allowed women and girls to work at night.

In June and July 1916 a threatened strike seemed likely to make matters worse. In the face of rising food prices (see Chapter 5) the weavers demanded a wage increase of 10 per cent and an extra halfpenny per hour for working without a creeler. In negotiations, the employers demanded that the Weavers' Association relax the rules on youths being employed on looms, and insisted that any increase in pay was considered a war bonus, only payable for the duration of the war and three months afterwards. Herbert Smith was the first of the employers to agree to the weavers' demands, and the others followed suit. The employers' demands were also agreed. Thereafter the war bonus steadily increased until, in October 1918, it reached 75 per cent of the pre-war wage.

Allowing youths of 18 to take charge of looms was the first manifestation of the 'dilution' of labour in the industry, a process whereby less skilled workers, mainly women, boys and unskilled men ineligible for the army, took over skilled jobs. In 1917 the Weavers' Association admitted women for the first time.

By the end of 1915, shortage of materials was blamed for reduced working hours, although business prospects were improving. Weavers and creelers were paid piece work, so a shortage of materials meant a loss of wages. Indian jute was vital as it formed the backing and framework of the carpets. However, it was also used to make the sandbags that shored up and protected trenches and other military emplacements. The jute manufacturers of Dundee

28. Tomkinson & Adam: Number of Employees. At Tomkinson & Adam about 75 per cent of the workforce was female throughout the war, but the number of both men and women fell to almost half the pre-war level.

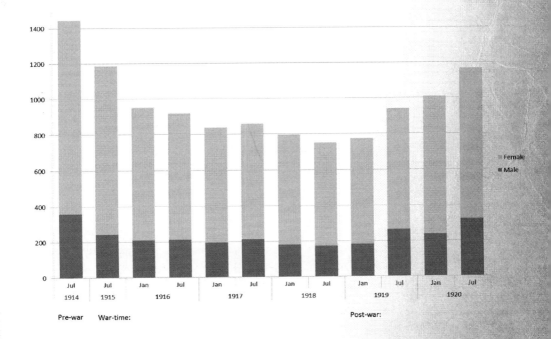

were ordered to produce 40 million sandbags during 1915 alone. Jute prices increased, and shortages for Kidderminster's carpet makers were prevalent thereafter. Wool was also needed for the war effort, especially soldiers' clothing and bedding. In June 1916, sheep-shearing time, the government issued an order prohibiting the sale of wool and commandeering the entire wool clip in England and Wales. The Kidderminster branch of the National Farmers Union forecast hardships 'unless steps are at once taken to secure that immediate payment shall be made at prices equal to those that would have been obtained in the open market.'

In 1916 colonial wool was still available, and in July 117,000 bales were auctioned. However, by 1917, these wools had also been commandeered. By spring 1918 shortages were becoming acute. There was a total loss of linen supplies, a reduction in jute, economies necessary with labour and coal, and it was expected that wool supplies would worsen.

War also stopped the supply of synthetic dyestuffs, since 90 per cent had been imported from Germany. Within six months aniline dyes were being purchased from a Swiss manufacturer using a government loan. In 1915 British Dyes Ltd was created to increase manufacture for the domestic carpet industry and Kidderminster firms bought shares.

In the face of reduced orders there were two obvious options for local manufacturers: they could contract with the government to make and supply items needed for the war effort, or they could make carpets for the export market. Making blankets and other materials needed for the war effort provided work and a more certain income when the carpet industry was struggling. However, it required the expense of adapting looms or buying new machinery, which was something of a gamble as demand would cease when the war ended and no one knew how long it would last. However, patriotism was an important motivator.

An intimation of the high demand for blankets came in October 1914 when Attwood & Isaac, at Regent House, advertised a stock of blankets, sheets and quilts available for the men billeted in the town. Nationally, before the war, just under 166,000 blankets had been produced each year; by 1918 production exceeded 16 million.

Not only Kidderminster, but other textile towns were involved (Fact box 13). By January 1915, only five months into the war, Naylor's was making blankets for the War Office (29–36). Its employees were working overtime, and a number were granted exemptions by the borough tribunal. They included C.J. Worthy of Plimsoll Street, a blanket tenterer – a new occupation required for saddle blankets which needed tentering more than ordinary army blankets.

By 1916 Naylor's were being pressurised to increase production, and needed their men to complete two large government contracts. They were also expecting to receive contracts for the allies. Their looms were running day and night, including Sundays, producing army blankets and saddle rugs. As much as 90 per cent of the production of the firm was for the government. Of their ninety-nine male employees, only twelve were fit for military service and all were necessary for government contracts.

Naylor's received a setback in January 1915 when there was a fire at Pike Mills. Nearby carpet company fire brigades attended, but the Willey shed was ruined, with damage estimated at about £3,000. This may have prompted Naylor's to start the process of moving to another site where they could build a new and safer factory. They also wanted to expand, and blanket production provided the initial impetus. In 1916 they acquired land between Green Street and Back Brook. A condition of the sale was that, within twelve months, a factory costing at least £1,000 for the manufacture of carpets, rugs or other fabrics should be erected on the site. By the end of the war, production facilities for white blankets had been established. This was the start of the Lowland Mills.

Fact box 13

DEFINITION OF MUNITIONS WORK, 1916
The manufacture or repair of:
- Arms, ammunition, ships, vessels, vehicles, and aircraft and any other articles intended or adapted for use in war.
- Any metals, machines or tools required for such manufacture.
- The materials required for such manufacture.

And:
- The supply of light, heat, water or power or the supply of tramways facilities for the purpose of carrying on munitions work, and the erection of buildings, machinery and plant for such supply.

Therefore, 'munitions work' included the making of army blankets.

Photographs showing the stages of blanket making at T&A Naylor Ltd. There are very few, if any, military age men visible, and women were employed to weave the blankets, which were despatched by horse transport. (Carpet Museum Trust)

29. *Carding the wool.*

30. *Mule spinning.*

31. *Weaving.*

32. *Scouring.*

33. *Drying.*

34. *Raising.*

35. *Packing.*

36. *Despatch.*

Other carpet firms produced materials for the forces: Cooke Brothers produced blankets; Brinton's produced blankets and webbing; and Herbert Smith explained to the borough tribunal in June 1916 that at his firm of Humphries & Sons, in Dixon Street 'much additional machinery was being erected … in order to fulfil government contracts for gun wads' and unless he could have the men he had claimed for it would not be possible to carry on some sections of the industry.

Not all of the firms supplying blankets for the war effort were spinning their own yarn. Hence, the government had to purchase from the spinners as well as the weaving firms. In 1916

Greatwich, 'greatly pressed by government orders', sought exemptions from service for George Rainsford, the firm's accountant and confidential clerk, and H.M. Westcott, the wool buyer and director of the mills, which employed 130 hands on 2,000 spindles. Only Westcott was exempted. In March 1917 Greatwich built an extension to their wool warehouse at a cost of £398 10s. The building was of 'Temporary character ... the plant also being an emergency one installed at inflated war cost to meet urgent army needs.'

The Hoobrook Spinning Company was also making yarns for army blankets. As it was outside of the borough, it successfully applied to the rural tribunal for the exemption of four key workers, three of whom were from the Hartland family. The spinning mills of E.A. Broome & Sons, were under government control because 75 per cent of their work was for the army, and Watson Brothers were running over 2,000 spindles, 77 per cent of which were working on government orders.

In April 1917 the local tribunal was criticised in the *London Daily Mail* for the number of exemptions granted to men on the firms' lists submitted for exemption (Fact box 14). It is impossible to judge whether the criticisms were justified: although the firms of the chairman and vice chairman of the tribunal had high numbers of exemptions, they were also among the largest employers in the area.

Fact box 14

CARPET FIRMS' LISTS PRESENTED TO THE BOROUGH TRIBUNAL

Number of men given temporary exemptions (numbers in brackets 'not assented to', or adjourned):

	October 1916	April 1917
Brinton's	13 (3)	15 (1)
Woodward Grosvenor	6 (1)	6 (2)
Tomkinson & Adam	16 (2)	17 (1)
Cooke Brothers	10	3
Carpet Manufacturing Co.	6 (2)	13 (4)
Chlidema	3 (1)	4
Hoobrook	4 (1)	3 (1)
Empire	3	6
Greatwich	9 (1)	9
Lea	8	11
Watson	16 (3)	11
Humphries	7 (1)	2
Hughes	8	5 (2)
Naylor	12 (2)	12 (1)
Jelleyman	5	5
Kidderminster Spinning	6	4
Victoria	11 (6)	16 (1)
Broome	–	4

Totals:

Applications	143	146
Exemptions	120	133
Not assented to/adjourned	23	13

In November 1917 the borough tribunal concluded that no more men could be secured for the army from the carpet and spinning trades. However, in 1918 there was a desperate need for men in the forces, and rumours circulated that there were hundreds of men employed in the carpet industry who should be in the army. Under the Manpower Act of April 1918 exemption certificates given on occupational grounds were withdrawn, and young men in non-essential industries were not be granted exemptions under any circumstances. Brinton commented that: 'If you take the head dyer for the army there is no need to take the other men into consideration – you may as well take the whole lot, and the firm will be closed.' Of the 102 local men that this order affected thirty-six were spinners doing government work, five were weavers and eighteen were working on government blankets at Naylor's.

There was a desperate need for artillery shells and so carpet firms' mechanics were pressed into producing small quantities. Brinton's loom tuner, T. Ward, of Castle Road, and two other mechanics worked on shells, and Tomkinson & Adam had three employees doing several processes for 4.5in shells.

The firms that chose to continue making carpets looked to the export market for orders. Nationally, carpet exports halved during the first four months of the war. The Colonies, South America and United States remained good customers, but trade with other countries was considerably reduced. Many local firms adapted part of their works for war production while continuing to produce carpets for export, thereby retaining a foothold in the future peacetime economy. Brinton's continued to produce Axminster carpets for export, and claimed that if their weavers were taken away £2,000–£3,000 worth of orders from neutral countries and the USA would be lost.

The Carpet Manufacturing Company also cultivated its export markets. In April 1916 Phillip Stokes, carpet traveller, was given four months exemption from military service to enable him to travel to Canada and America. He made a second trip before enlisting in the Inns of Court Corps. Naylor's also attempted to retain a foothold in the export market, even though carpets were only about 10 per cent of its output. Their only remaining designer, Walter Shepherd, who had studied at Kidderminster School of Art and was working on new designs for the export trade, was granted a conditional exemption only after an appeal. He was working on a patent cloth which no other firm was making.

The Victoria Carpet Company claimed that the absence of their starcher, William Henry Styles, would cause a reduction in production to the detriment of the weavers and the export trade. In response to the two months' exemption that was granted, Mr Anton, director, claimed it would be impossible to get another man and if the starching was hampered then the work of 250 people would be affected. Brinton retorted, 'The carpet industry may not be running then.'

Tomkinson & Adam did not take on any government contracts, but continued to put their efforts into carpet production, particularly exports. The firm repeatedly reported that trade was quiet from May 1916 to the end of the year, blaming shortages of materials and labour. However, in January 1917 business prospects were so improved that they could not execute even the export orders on their books, although these were being given preference. The factory was now operating the full fifty-five and a half hour week, and many men were regularly working eight hours' overtime. Despite this, half their plant was idle, needing more than 600 additional employees to bring it into operation.

Shipping, essential for export and the importation of raw materials, faced great hazards. The Germans appreciated Britain's need for both food and industrial raw materials, and their U-boats attacked all merchant ships inside their definition of British waters. International maritime law protecting merchant shipping was ignored by the Germans who, in February 1917, launched a submarine offensive, and shipping losses soared. They were only reduced with the introduction of the convoy system in June but, by then U-boats had created serious shortages in many areas of the economy.

The carpet industry was forced to turn to the domestic market which, although declining, had not been totally neglected.

The Carpet Manufacturing Company planned new showrooms and stores in New Road. By July 1917 only 40 per cent of Tomkinson's output was for the export market. Finally, in the latter half of 1918, Tomkinson's realised that supplying the war effort might be good for business and informed the government: 'We are shortly submitting samples of flannel which we hope to be able to produce for government use.' Shortly afterwards peace arrived in November!

Lloyd George, then chancellor, visiting France in mid-October 1914, learned of the surprisingly large amount of artillery ammunition which was being expended. Previously, battles had been short followed by a period of calm in which to regroup. In France men had already been fighting for seventy-nine days with the great cannon firing almost night and day. In only two weeks fighting around Neuve Chappelle, almost as much artillery ammunition had been used as during the three years of the Boer War. He quickly grasped the implications and, in February 1915, called for the mobilisation of industry. By September he realised that unskilled men and women would need to be employed to achieve the level of output required.

Fact box 15

MUNITIONS OF WAR ACTS, 1915
The Acts made provision for:
- The arbitration of trade disputes, where manufacture or supply of war materials is involved, with the decision binding on both parties.
- The Minister of Munitions to declare any establishment in which munitions work is carried out to be a controlled establishment and subject to regulations made by the minister.
- The authorisation of the wearing of badges by persons engaged on munitions work.

This abrupt increase in demand, forcing the government to buy all available supplies, meant that prices soared leading to accusations of war profiteering. In response, munitions factories were taken under government control (Fact box 15), prices were controlled, an excess profits tax was introduced, and the country was divided into areas, each overseen by a Munitions Committee. Kidderminster came under the Birmingham Munitions Committee, which received orders from the government and distributed each order among the manufacturers of the district. At the same time existing armaments factories were expanded, new factories were built, and other engineering firms were converted to armaments production for the first time.

In Kidderminster there were three main armaments manufacturers: Baldwin's, at the Stour Vale Iron Works to the north of the town next to the canal; Bradley & Turton's, who had foundries at Caldwell and Clensmore; and the Castle Motor Co., whose works were in New Road.

Baldwin's strongly supported the war effort, and encouraged men from all of their factories, including the Stour Vale Works, to enlist by offering financial help to their wives of 10s per week plus an additional 1s for each child under 14. It was estimated that this would cost the company approaching £8,000 a year. In the first twelve weeks of the war 674 of their men had enlisted. By October 1916, over 1,200 of their employees had enlisted of whom seventy-one 'had fallen gloriously' and sixty-four had been wounded. The company contributed about £1,000 to the Prince of Wales' Fund and the Belgian Relief Fund. In addition, they handed over one of their large engineering shops to the Ministry of Munitions, free of charge, for the manufacture of high explosive shells. They expanded rapidly during the war in an attempt to own and control as much of the process of production as possible, and avoid the rapidly rising prices of pig iron and coal. In spite of the excess profits tax of 80 per cent, Baldwin's flourished.

Bradley & Turton came under government control early in the war. In 1916 they built a new munitions shop, which was ready by May when the company started producing substantial quantities of blank shells, almost certainly in preparation for the Somme offensive of July. In June, alterations were made to the shell shop and to the lavatories and mess room, perhaps to accommodate women workers. By the end of October, 9,438 shells had been produced at a cost of 5s 6d per shell. Another 3,588 had been 'nosed' at a cost of 3d each and a further 1,200 defective shells had been made good during the same period. By the end of June 1917 Bradley & Turton had charged the Birmingham Munitions Committee £7,704 for 35,500 shells. They also manufactured essential spares and components for other companies engaged in war work including local carpet companies, other engineering firms, and the suppliers of essential services such as collieries, gas suppliers, the post office and the tram and train companies.

The Castle Motor Company also produced armaments (37). Fifty-three men were employed in the munitions department by 1916, working in two shifts (38). In an effort to get enough labour part-time workers were employed: W.J. Slater was a member of the band at the Opera House and, in his spare time, worked as a shell turner. Responding to the local paper which

37. *Shells ready for despatch at the Castle Motor Company. Notice the young lads in the background.* (Robert Barber)

38. *Armaments workshop at the Castle Motor Company, showing the belts that transferred the power from the turning shaft overhead to the machinery on the benches.* (Robert Barber)

claimed that many of their employees were single men who should be in the army, Stanley Goodwin, managing director, said in June 1916 that there were only five single men, and that the firm was 'engaged on important government contracts which cannot be delayed, but, nevertheless, arrangements are being carried out for the proper accommodation of female workers, whom we hope to employ as soon as possible, for the purpose of releasing the few eligible men mentioned for the army' (39).

By the end of the war their munitions department had produced over 160,000 base plates for shells, 83,000 4.5in shells, and 6,000 pistols for detonating depth charges, as well as aeroplane engine valves and hubs for artillery guns and limbers. The company also continued to operate its automotive repair department, in spite of the loss of forty-one skilled men. The work was mostly repairing commercial lorries, doctors' cars, and vehicles used by employers engaged on government contracts.

Edwin Preston's brass and iron foundry in Park Lane provided iron and moulded iron components (including special fire bars for warships) for the munitions manufacturers who did not have their own foundries. Before the war, Preston's iron moulders had been paid 32s per week but by 1918 war bonuses had almost doubled their wage to 59s 6d for a fifty-four hour week. Nevertheless, by April 1918, their union, the Friendly Society of Iron Founders, had gone to arbitration for an additional 8s a week, and a reduction of one hour in the working week. Munitions work was lucrative; in 1919 Charles Leonard Wall, head gardener at Gordon Smith's with four or five men working under him, earned £2 10s a week, but when working in munitions he had earned £5 or more a week.

The production and transport of munitions required a lot of supporting work, which the government also had to commission. For example, Harry Simmonds of Jerusalem Walk, timber sawyer at Bateman's steam saw mills, cut the timber used in making munitions packing cases. S.J. Collins, of St George's Terrace, was a haulier and haulage contractor using motor wagons and horses to transport munitions from Cookley ironworks to Kidderminster railway station seven days a week. In April 1917 he purchased another, second-hand, motor wagon for this work. However, it could not carry 3 tons up the one-in-four gradient of Station Hill. While it was being overhauled 'many tons of unfinished work have accumulated at the works and [Collins] has been threatened with all kinds of pains and penalties both by the manufacturers and by government officials.'

Coal was also essential for the war effort: Mr Wright, chandler, applied for exemption for W.H. Birch, of Wood Lane in Hurcott, who made candles for controlled collieries. The tribunal chairman suggested that a girl could easily cut candle wicks and Wright replied that a girl would cut a sorry figure at the job, but exemption was still refused.

In all areas of work the demand for labour outstripped supply. Four to five thousand men went into the armed forces from Kidderminster, over half of the male working age population. This loss of labour was accompanied by the additional demands of wartime production. Women filled some of these gaps, but many women were already employed by the carpet industry. Therefore, other ways had to be found to increase both labour and output.

In February 1916, parents were informed that arrangements had been made to hold an additional examination for Labour Certificates at Coventry Street Boys School. Children aged 13 or over were to be examined, 'for whom employment may be desired before they reach the age of 14.' In September it was reported that there was a large falling off in attendance at elementary and Sunday schools. Even where children were not employed themselves, absent or working parents meant they needed to take more responsibility in the home. Schoolchildren could be put to work in other ways too – in late 1917 schoolboys made a house to house collection of domestic scrap metal for making war materials.

Another solution was having more than one job: H. Miles Waite, the licensed victualler of the Railway Train Inn in Offmore Road, polished shells at night at the Castle Motor Company. He had been asked to work full-time on shells but was quite satisfied with his work and pay and did not take up the offer.

40 Kidderminster people wanted to take advantage of the number of visitors to the town over the revised bank holiday, as this advert from September 1916 shows, but there was also hostility to the men they thought should be in the army. (Kidderminster Shuttle)

WHERE EVERYBODY GOES.

To Lodging-House Keepers and others.

HOLIDAYS having been arranged for Munition workers from September 28th to October 1st, and a large influx of visitors from Birmingham and other Midland Munition Areas being probable, PERSONS desiring to PROVIDE LODGINGS and other accommodation for such visitors, are invited to send FULL PARTICULARS thereof, including Tariffs, with a Registration Fee of 1s., to the TOWN CLERK'S OFFICE, Kidderminster. Steps will be taken to bring the accommodation in Kidderminster to the notice of intending visitors.
9188

In 1916 the government and the unions recommended that the early June Whitsun bank holiday for munition workers be postponed for two months in order to maintain output. Again, with hindsight, it can be seen that this was in preparation for the Somme offensive to be launched in July. In support of the munition workers it was agreed that the shops in the borough would remain open on Whit Monday and Tuesday, and there would be no holidays in the elementary schools. The press commented that: 'Not within the memory of anyone living has such a Whitsuntide been experienced as this week, all the elementary schools were open, and most of the tradesmen's establishments in the town transacted business as usual'.

Not everyone was filled with patriotic fervour. At a meeting in late June, when the weavers discussed the stopping of the bank holiday, Mr Stradling claimed that the workers 'had been filched of their liberty by the capitalists. Let them keep their eye on the next bank holiday, and, if the manufacturers attempt anything of the sort in the same way, the weavers will teach them a lesson.' He did not carry out his threat, for the August bank holiday was also cancelled. It was thought imperative that there was no reduction in the output of munitions and a holiday atmosphere should be avoided. Nevertheless, the town became crowded with people from the Black Country and Birmingham, both at Whitsuntide and the revised bank holiday of 28 September– 1 October 1916 (40).

There was resentment, among tribunal members, of the protected munitions workers and Tomkinson referred to 'skulking single men who were protecting themselves in munitions works'. In response to the influx of young men to Kidderminster on the cancelled Whit holiday, the borough tribunal resolved that it:

Views with dissatisfaction the large number of young men apparently employed in munition works in the Midlands and exempted from Military Service; and respectfully suggests to the Ministry of Munitions that much more may yet be done in the way of 'combing out' and replacing the young men by the medically unfit or men passed for sedentary occupation, and generally by women and older men.

Copies were sent to the Secretary of State for War, the Minister of Munitions and various local MPs. In response, 'one of the munition shirkers', of Hall Green, Birmingham, wrote that he thought:

> A certain class of residents would like all munition workers to have no recreation whatever, as the majority of their own kinsfolk are serving with the forces. My only regret is that Kidderminster should have been the spot chosen by munition workers for their leisure hours, which are rather few, excepting weekends … they have no desire to escape military service. But we are, and always will be, accused of having hid ourselves behind munitions while others fought for us.

The following week 'one who knows' replied:

> I take [it] 'Hall Green' is a skilled workman, if so he is not wanted in the army, and he is doing his bit, but if not he ought to be fighting. I can take him … between here and Birmingham and Coventry and find enough men to raise two or more regiments who before the war broke out never knew what work was … I can find him … every kind of workman excepting skilled who sneaked inside not to join the army.

The Tribunal Advisory Committee appointed a subcommittee to go through the lists of ineligible employees in the various factories, and local manufacturers agreed to inform recruiting officers within three days of any men leaving their employment, and not to engage men of military age without consulting the military officer of the district. The authorities inspected the certificates of exemption of over 200 young men in the locality.

All were satisfactory. This was not the 'combing out' that the tribunal wanted.

In May 1917, Sydney Campbell's application for exemption led to a further outburst against young male munition workers. He was a 41-year-old foundry worker. A number of young men working at the foundry had been badged, while he had been overlooked. A military representative visited the foundry, which employed twenty-two men under 25 years of age, eighteen of whom were single. They had been de-badged, and would soon be before the tribunal. From late 1917 the tribunal's hostility appears to have led to them to refuse exemption for almost all munition workers who came before them.

Kidderminster also supported the war effort by treating and caring for wounded soldiers. The town's existing infirmary, had difficulty maintaining sufficient expertise during the war. Dr Bertram Addenbrooke was appointed surgeon major to the 7th Worcesters, and went to France in early in 1915. After six months he was transferred to the General Hospital at Rouen. He was later demobilised due to ill health and arrived home in October 1917. By 1916, Homfray Addenbrooke had died, Walter Moore was no longer at the infirmary and Samuel Stretton, although still listed as a consulting surgeon, was in his 80s, and his son Lionel had taken over as leading surgeon at the infirmary. The house surgeon's post remained unfilled and other specialist support was difficult to obtain.

As employment opportunities expanded during the war so staffing the infirmary became more difficult. In August 1915 a laundress who was a good washer and ironer was required to head a team of three in the hand laundry, for a salary of £22 per annum plus material for a uniform. Maids were offered a salary of £12–£15 per annum. Exemptions were sought for staff of military age, including Arthur Glizzard of Sambourne, a male nurse. In September 1916, H. Bunn retired aged 70, after forty-four years at the infirmary – the advertisement for a good strong youth, about 16, to assist the porter may have been the attempt to replace him and the invitation for applicants to state the wages required is indicative of the problems in the employment market.

Demand for the infirmary's services was strong and increasing. Before the war there had been an average of forty inpatients at any one time and by 1915 it was over fifty. Outpatient attendances increased from about 500 per month to over 800 in August 1916. Small numbers of injured soldiers were being treated from early in the war and, in April 1915, there were two soldier patients. Lieutenant Arthur Davis was admitted as a private patient at the expense of Mrs Griffith Williams of the Vicarage in Chaddesley Corbett at £3 3s per week. In February 1916 five soldiers were treated as paying patients in the infirmary.

Doctor Stretton attributed the increase in work partly to the treatment of wounded soldiers, but mainly to the general amount of illness owing to lower vitality caused by the effects of the war. However, the increased prosperity of the town (see Chapter 5) may also have meant that more people could afford medical treatment, and the demands of the new industries and expanded workforce may have increased the need.

An additional burden came in August 1916 when, in response to an urgent appeal by the military authorities, twenty beds at the infirmary were made available for wounded soldiers requiring surgery. Lieutenant George E. Pitt, of the Middlesex Regiment, visited the town to give a lecture on 'Experiences amongst the French' and raise money for the provision of these beds. His lecture raised £21 2s 5d. Wounded soldiers were already receiving treatment at the infirmary with no government financial assistance, and the grant of £1 10s a week eventually received for each soldier did not cover the full cost of £1 15s 3d a week, so local supporters of the infirmary helped to meet the shortfall. By 1918, the infirmary was treating an average of twenty-four seriously wounded soldiers at any one time, increasing the total number of inpatients by almost half.

Miss Hilda Bell, a volunteer masseuse, attended the infirmary every day for three years to treat the wounded soldiers.

As well as injury, soldiers were vulnerable to venereal diseases and by 1916, under Dr Lionel Stretton, the infirmary was treating sufferers. Defence of the Realm legislation, of March 1918, made it an offence for a woman to pass on a venereal disease to a serviceman, while the army adopted the euphemism 'sick through negligence' for the 60,000 servicemen infected. Worcestershire County Council asked the infirmary to be the county centre for treating venereal diseases, and Stretton became the medical officer in charge.

Before the war the infirmary had been running at an annual financial deficit, and this was exacerbated by the war. The £4,400 spent during 1915 exceeded income by £639. The financial position of the infirmary was unsatisfactory. A year later, there was an appeal to residents to help remove the infirmary's heavy debt, which stood at over £2,000. Donations of up to £100 were made to the deficit fund by local residents and businesses, and the Weavers Association made a special donation of £10 10s. Throughout the war fundraising for the infirmary was extremely important. Subscriptions and Saturday collections continued, and in December 1915 a 'Grateful Patients' Day' was held, when former patients showed their gratitude by contributing small sums. In March 1916 the infirmary made an emotional appeal for help to clear the pre-war debt through a 'Shilling Fund': 'Discharged soldiers in large numbers will need treatment after the war is ended, and even earlier. Can we refuse treatment to the heroes who have fought for us? Certainly not!'

Donors came from as far afield as Ombersley, Kinlet and Alveley. In its first month the appeal raised £20 17s 8d. Other events were organised to raise funds and 'Pound Days' were very successful – visitors donated a pound weight (lb) of goods or a pound in money, and were able to tour the wards and the nurses' home. On the two Pound Days held in April 1916 they received £144 in money and 9,335¾lb weight of groceries, which included 6,720lb coal and 453lb potatoes, together with large amounts of jam, soap, parsnips, apples, bottled fruit and oranges.

However, costs continued to increase at an alarming rate. By 1917 they had reached £6,550. Although more work was being done, particularly for the soldiers, the prices of food and medical

supplies were abnormally high. Tensions developed between management and the doctors, and public confidence suffered. In effect, the infirmary ran out of money in 1918. By then the weekly cost of a patient was at least 2 guineas. A further appeal was launched, but only £149 was given or promised.

41. The Larches, built c. 1825, had twelve bedrooms, a number of other rooms, outhouses with accommodation above, and a 23 acre estate. It had been for sale in 1913. (Kidderminster Civic Society)

There was also an appeal for anyone with extra food that might have been 'inadvertently hoarded' to donate it to the infirmary, giving the guilty the chance to avoid a formal enquiry. Two weeks later the list of gifts received included several pounds of butter, tea and sugar and 28lb of jam, as well as a piano, a cot and six dozen bottles of stout from Kidderminster Brewery.

From the start of the war numbers of wounded were expected to be greater than existing hospitals could cope with. The British Red Cross Society prepared to nurse the wounded, and looked for premises in England to use as temporary hospitals. The first local soldiers' hospital was created at Wynn Cottages in Wribbenhall, where eight beds were provided for nursing all the county's convalescents from the war. No one yet realised just how many casualties there would be.

In Kidderminster, a hospital was set up at the Beeches, in Franche, for the 7th Worcesters by a Women's Red Cross Voluntary Aid Detachment (Fact box 16). The house was owned by Michael Tomkinson. In the first nine months of the war ninety-five inpatients and 291 outpatients were treated there, but this too was inadequate. In March 1915 the Red Cross started to fit out the Larches, in Foley Park, as a hospital (41). Until recently the home of carpet magnate Sir Sidney Lea, it had a large number of rooms and extensive grounds making it ideal accommodation for large numbers of convalescing soldiers. Furniture was brought from the Beeches, and 100 beds were installed at the Larches under the guidance of hospital Commandant Marion Tomkinson, daughter of Michael and his wife, Anne. The first twenty wounded soldiers arrived at the end of May, and by 5 June there were fifty patients at the hospital, including twelve New Zealanders.

The Larches remained open until 30 April 1919, by which time 2,278 inpatients and many outpatients had been treated there. Most were not local men, since the wounded were sent wherever there were vacant beds. However, two local men are known to have been treated there: Gunner H. Walters of the 2nd South Midland Brigade Royal Field Artillery arrived in July 1916. His mother lived in Crowther Street. He was just 21 and had been an Axminster weaver at Brinton's. Lance Corporal G.E. Postings, whose parents lived in Arch Hill Square, was recovering from wounds received on 9 August 1916. He had worked at the railway station until joining the army five months previously. He had married in May.

Tribunal proceedings at the Town Hall on 26 September 1917 were interrupted to present the Distinguished Conduct Medal to Sergeant William James Collins of the 8th Battalion, York and Lancaster Regiment, who was then convalescing

Fact box 16

VOLUNTARY AID DETACHMENTS (VADS) IN WORCESTERSHIRE, MARCH 1916

23 Women's VADs:

Number of women	1,189
Number of beds	883
Number of patients treated	4,653

6 Men's VADs:

Number of men	86

Additional VADs were still being formed.

at The Larches. Many of his fellow patients and the commandant of the hospital attended the ceremony. The Mayor of Kidderminster, J.H. Watson, pinned the medal to his chest.

As far as Kidderminster people were concerned it did not matter that the patients were not local, they were wounded heroes who deserved all the help and support that could be given. This support often took the form of organised entertainments, outings, gifts and fundraising events. In August 1915 Brinton published an:

Appeal against the practice which seems to have been springing up recently of surreptitious treating of wounded soldiers. While one can appreciate the under lying sympathy which prompts the action ... alcohol is absolutely forbidden to convalescents; and in some cases this 'treating' has been proved to be very harmful to the patient's progress. Any soldier in hospital who is found the worse for drink is sent back to Birmingham, which involves both disgrace and the stoppage of furlough ...

Fact box 17

DONATIONS TO THE LARCHES, RED CROSS HOSPITAL

Donors included:

Wribbenhall School, Foley Park School, St Mary's School, Lea Street School, Mrs Gardiner, The Rev. Mother Superior at Elderslie, Mrs Cooke of the Lakes, Miss R. Smith, Mr H. Winbury, Mr J. Tomkinson, Captain Squire, Mrs Isaac, Miss D. Butcher, Mr Saywin Lucas, Mrs Cartmale, Mrs Davies of Wolverley, Mrs Anton, Mrs W. Adam, Mrs Reeve, Mrs Austin, Mrs Beveridge of Trimpley, The Women's Liberal Association, Mrs A. Naylor, Mrs Jerome, Mrs Goodwin, Mrs Tomkinson.

Gifts regularly received included:

Seasonal fruit and vegetables

Bread, Eggs, Butter, Jam, Flour, Books, Magazines, Cigarettes.

Other gifts included:

A croquet set, bed socks, billiard balls and cues from the Workmen's Club, a set of bowls, croquet balls, rabbits, a thermometer, the washing of nightshirts, gramophone records, shirts from the Midland Counties Needlework Guild.

In 1916 Mr Reynolds gave the Larches a cricket bat, leg guards and bag, while the committee of Kidderminster Cricket Club donated wickets, and on 3 June the patients challenged the nurses to play them at cricket (42). Is this one of the earliest women's cricket teams?

42. The scorecard for the cricket match played at the Larches between the staff (N=Nurse) and patients, privates and non-commissioned officers, in June 1916. (Kidderminster Shuttle)

The many gifts from schools, local firms and numerous individuals were acknowledged through the local paper (Fact box 17). At a Pound Day in June 1915 over 2,000 people, including many school children, visited the Larches bringing over 2,000lb of goods as donations.

Concern for the wounded manifested itself in other ways: in 1915 a Disabled Soldiers' Fund was started to enable men with artificial limbs to be taught a trade after the war; in 1917, a blind representative of St Dunstan's House visited local carpet works and addressed the Baxter Church congregation; four

THE STAFF.

N. Crane, c Moules, b Bagnall	0
Matron, c Moules, b Bagnall	0
Commandant, c Bagnall, b Robbie	1
N. M. Tomkinson, c Foxall, b Bagnall	1
N. Goodwin, c Foxall. b Bagnall	0
N. Wilson, b Bagnall	12
N. Adam, c Castle, b Bagnall	7
N. C. Tomkinson, c and b Castle	1
N. Brinton, b Bagnall	0
N. Simpson, b Castle	1
N. Acton, not out	0
Total	**23**

THE PATIENTS.

Pte. Robbie, b Wilson	4
Gr. Foxall, c and b Wilson	5
Pte. Smith, b Anton	4
Pte. Bagnall, b Wilson	0
Pte. Moules, c Adam, b Anton	13
Sergt. Castle, b Wilson	3
Lce.-Corpl. Bolland, c Goodwin, b Wilson	0
Pte. Hay, st Goodwin, b Anton	2
Pte. Cattermole, c Anton, b Wilson	1
Pte. Sutton, b Wilson	2
Lce.-Corpl. Woodford, not out	6
Byes	3
Total	**43**

substantially made seats, inscribed 'For Wounded Soldiers', were placed in front of the Town Hall – they were patronised mainly by women and children waiting for motor buses, but also by the soldiers for whom they were intended. By 1918 ambulance classes were held weekly in the Town Hall, and home nursing classes for both men and women were advertised. Many ill and injured men who needed nursing were already returning home (Profile 4).

LAURA BELL'S WAR

In November 1914, three months after the outbreak of war, Laura Bennett married Samuel Frederick Bell (10). She was a 26-year-old carpet passer who lived with her mother in Stourbridge Road. Her husband, aged 27, was a commercial traveller of George Street. The couple moved to Worcester.

A year after their marriage Samuel enlisted and, as Gunner Bell, served in the Royal Field Artillery in Salonika and Egypt. Laura returned to her family home in Stourbridge Road.

As the illustration shows, she took the opportunity offered by the buoyant employment market and in May 1917, she was issued with a Motor Omnibus Conductor's License by the borough council. A manually altered Hackney Carriage Drivers' License was used, signed by Spencer Thursfield. By then, most of the conductors on local trams and buses were women.

Her husband, Samuel, contracted malaria in September 1917, to which was added anaemia in 1918. He returned to his wife's home in Kidderminster a sick man. As his malaria and 30 per cent debility both resulted from his war service, he was awarded a weekly pension of 9s 11d.

The couple moved to Smethwick in the Black Country. However, Samuel died in October 1920 in the Ministry of Pensions Hospital, Ruskin Park, London. He was buried in Kidderminster cemetery. The family documents include a bill for a pair of corsets purchased by Laura in London in 1920, perhaps while she was visiting her husband in hospital.

She received an army widow's pension of 20s a week, and went to live with her sister-in-law, Jane Taylor nèe Bell, and her husband in Chester Road, Kidderminster. Laura had been married for six years but had only spent two and a half years with her husband, who had been ill for eighteen months of that time.

Samuel's name is on the Kidderminster war memorial.

449

BOROUGH OF KIDDERMINSTER.
HACKNEY CARRIAGES.

Driver's License.

motor *omnibus*

Badge No. *omnibus*

This is to certify that the Council of the Borough of Kidderminster do hereby license *Laura Bell*
204 Stourbridge Road.

to act as Driver of any Hackney Carriage plying for Hire within the said Borough, under and subject to the Orders, Rules, Regulations, and Bye-Laws from time to time in force, and to the Statutes made and provided. This License to be in force from the day of the date hereof until the Ninth day of November, 1917

Dated this 21st day of May 19 17

By order of the Watch Committee appointed by the Council,

Spencer Thursfield
Deputy . Town Clerk.

N.B.—This License is to be retained by the Driver of the Carriage and to be produced and exhibited, on demand, to any person hiring such Carriage or to the Inspector of Hackney Carriages, or to any Constable of the Borough. This License shall also be produced in all cases of complaint, where the Driver is summoned to attend before the Justices; and be given up to the Town Clerk on the Driver ceasing to act as such within the Borough.

4

NEWS FROM THE FRONT LINE

43. *Number of
deaths recorded in
the* Kidderminster
Shuttle *for each
month of the
Great War (by date
of death).*

Not only did local people see the injuries wrought by the war but,
through the press, they learned about the fighting and the deaths
as well. Letters from loved ones were published in the papers,
and many families (but not all) gave details of their deaths and
injuries to the press, including photographs. Almost 900 soldiers'
deaths are recorded in the *Kidderminster Shuttle*. Of these, just
under 500 are also named on the town's war memorials. Most

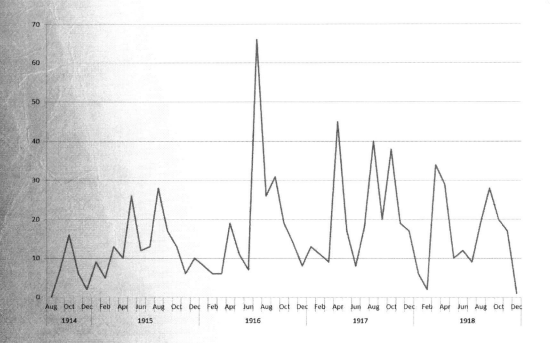

of the rest came from other towns and villages in the district. Graphical analysis (43) shows that the deaths of local people closely followed the national pattern, as they participated in the major battles of the war: Gallipolli in May and August 1915, the Somme in July 1916, Arras in April 1917, Passchendaele in August and October 1917, the German offensives of early 1918 and the final Allied offensive later in the year. At least one of the smaller battles, Katia in 1916, had a disproportionate local impact. It is the local experience of these battles that is considered in this chapter.

In January 1915 Russia, dealing with a Turkish attack in the Caucasus, requested a diversionary attack on Turkey. The only viable site was in the Dardanelles. After the Battle of Mons (see Chapter 1) the two sides in France had failed to outflank each other and had entrenched, reaching stalemate. Decisive manoeuvres had to be made elsewhere. The Dardanelles would provide a sea route to Russia, for war supplies, when Russia's northern ports were frozen.

An Allied naval operation was mounted by battleships, minesweepers, cruisers and destroyers. Their crews included Able Seamen Henry and Wilfred Jones, whose parents lived in Mason Road. The attack was defeated by the mobile shore guns of the Turks, and the density of sea mines. A land attack was needed to knock out the guns. Aware of Allied interest, the Turks strengthened their defences, protecting potential landing places with barbed wire and trenches. Landings were attempted at dawn on 25 April on five beaches on Cape Helles at the tip of the Gallipoli Peninsula. All were overlooked by higher land. Two landings were strongly opposed, with Turks shelling and machine-gunning the men as they approached the beaches. However, initial landings were made. The 4th Worcesters (including many Kidderminster men) followed, and were able to climb the adjacent hill. Two Turkish redoubts on top were protected by thick belts of barbed wire and passages were cut by men crawling beneath and cutting the wire above them, being replaced by colleagues when they were shot. The redoubts were eventually taken.

Casualties were heavy. Most were regular soldiers who had seen action in India and South Africa: Lance Corporal J. Hill, whose mother lived in New Road, and who had worked as a painter and decorator, died on 28 April; Private Harry Watkins, whose parents lived in Mill Lane, died on 30 April, having enlisted before the war; Sergeant Frederick Buckley, of New Road, was wounded on 11 May and died about three weeks later after being in the army for fourteen years; Private John Evans, previously a blacksmith's striker at Hughes' carpet firm, whose mother lived at Rock Terrace, was invalided home after the action, having spent five years in the army; and Private Sidney Andrews, whose father-in-law was W.H. Phipps of Offmore Road, and who had worked for Broome & Brookes, was reported missing from 6 August, and he was later assumed to have died. He had been married on the previous Christmas morning.

The attack is particularly known for the sacrifices of the Australia and New Zealand Army Corps (ANZACS), who suffered horrific casualties when they attempted to land. Among their number was Private W. Poyner who had emigrated to Australia just over two years previously to work on the railway service. He had enlisted at the outbreak of war and died on 2 May aged 22. His parents lived at Park Villas in Sutton Road. Private J.E. Pickard of the Wellington Regiment, New Zealand, also had relatives in Kidderminster who were informed of his death in May.

In August, another attempt was made at Suvla Point, about 10 miles north of the first landings. The landing forces were again penned close to the sea. They were strengthened by forces from Cape Helles but could make little headway. Private Alfred Davis of Mill Street, previously a horse keeper at Dalley's, died in the attack on 6 August, having been sent to the Dardanelles a month previously. He left a widow and seven children.

The Allies remained there, through a hot summer into a freezing winter. Private W. Tovey, only drafted to the Dardanelles in November, was wounded in December and suffered from dysentery. Private W. Humphries, whose parents lived in Park Street, was wounded in the leg and sent to hospital in Malta.

After a freak storm drowned soldiers in their trenches, the Gallipoli Peninsula was evacuated in late December and early January 1916. Casualties had been extremely heavy: the Turks lost about 300,000 killed and wounded, the Allies 265,000. The 29th Division, which included the 4th Worcesters, lost its strength twice over.

Turkish forces were also the enemy at the Battle of Katia on 23 April 1916. The defenders included the Worcestershire Yeomanry, which was like a Kidderminster 'pals battalion' (see Chapter 2) (44). The local impact of the battle far outweighed its national significance. In order to improve the defence of the Suez Canal, a crucial link with India and other parts of the Empire, it was decided to block access routes across the Sinai Desert which could be used by Turkish forces. One route was blocked by occupying oases in the Katia area, 30 miles east of the canal. In April 1916 the Worcestershire Yeomanry, Warwickshire Yeomanry and Gloucestershire Hussars occupied oases at Romani, Katia, Oghratina and Hamisah, supported by unmounted units but no artillery. There were about 1,500 men.

On Easter Sunday they were attacked by about 3,600 Turks under German command, with artillery support. Two squadrons of Worcestershire Yeomanry at Oghratina were attacked at 4.00 a.m. in thick fog. They were driven back, but were unable to withdraw without deserting their unmounted support. By 7.45 a.m. eleven officers and thirty-five other ranks were casualties and the remainder were compelled to surrender. A third squadron of Worcestershire Yeomanry was sent to reinforce the Gloucestershire Yeomanry, under attack at Katia. However, the camp was shelled and most of their horses killed or maimed, preventing them from retiring with the other regiments. Only a few men were able to get away, including 22-year-old Trooper Harry Morris, a scoutmaster in Kidderminster and employed

44. *Howard Tolley, aged 17, in the Worcestershire Yeomanry, on his horse, Blackie, in 1913. In October 1915 he joined the Worcestershire Regiment. He was demobilised in March 1919. (Bryan Tolley)*

by the Prudential. His parents lived in Crescent Road and in a letter home, he wrote, 'We have been through a terrible time, almost worse than Gallipoli. I got back with just the few clothes I stand in.'

The rest of the survivors had to surrender. After inflicting defeat the Turks withdrew, taking around 200 British captives with them. A letter from Farrier Major Lawley, of Bewdley, told of the prisoners' subsequent treatment:

> We have travelled a good many miles across the desert since my last letter. We are in a beautiful hospital now, nearly 100 of us at Damascus [300 miles from Katia]. This is the first proper hospital we have been in. Strange to say they are French Sisters of Mercy, but they are very good to us … We are allowed some tobacco and a little wine each day … This is a lovely place – beautiful gardens, trees loaded with apricots, peaches, etc.; but alas! we are prisoners. My wounds have practically got all right; many have to leave here to join the fit ones at some concentration camp. Don't worry, I can assure you our treatment is far above whatever my expectations were.

Another prisoner wrote appealing for food, especially tinned food, as they had to live off pearl barley, lentils and barley bread with no tea or any drink at all.

News of the battle was devastating for Kidderminster, so many of the dead and captured troopers came from the town. A number were local butchers. Trooper Percy Hanglin, secretary of the local Master Butchers' Association, had died in the action. After ten years' service his brother, Ernest, had rejoined the Yeomanry in September 1914, and died of wounds a few days after the battle. The parents of missing Trooper Charles Henry Rastall lived in Blackwell Street, where he had previously assisted his father in his butchers business. He was the servant of Lieutenant Sir John Henry Jaffray, who was also missing. Both men had died in the action.

Trooper Lionel Longmore, the youngest son of parents in Hill Grove Crescent, who had worked for R. Smith & Sons before enlisting, was reported missing. Trooper Gill eventually wrote from a prisoner-of-war camp that Longmore was killed trying to reach his pal, who was shot about 20 yards from him. Missing Trooper J.C. Probert, almost 19 years old having enlisted aged 17, had been employed in the Borough Surveyor's Office and his parents lived in Stourport Road. The wife of missing Trooper Charles S. Young lived in Park Street, and on the same morning that she heard her husband was missing their only child, a 3-year-old girl, died. He had been a foreman at Hopkins, Garlick & Co, brewers in Mill Street.

Major Eric Knight 'knew all of the officers and many of the men he had enlisted into the regiment, and that they should have been forced to surrender was a matter of the gravest sorrow to him'.

It took a long time to ascertain the fate of the missing troopers. The parents of Trooper Jack Harvey lived at Fairlawn, and heard in July that he was a prisoner of war at Hamadiah. However, in September they learned that he had died in May, after writing a last letter home. Missing Trooper Muntz Roden was later reported to have died. His parents lived in St George's Terrace, and he had married Eva Nicholls of Kidderminster a year previously. But in July, he wrote from Afion-Kara-Hissar that his wound was better and he was a prisoner of war receiving good treatment. His wife had already been in mourning for him.

In May, Stanley Baldwin attempted to help anxious relatives with questions in the House of Commons, but no information had been received. It was not until July that the Red Cross received a list of fifteen officers, one army priest, and 161 non-commissioned officers and men taken prisoner at Katia. The officers were interned at Angora (Ankara), 500 miles beyond Damascus, and the men at Afion-Kara-Hissar. A list of the names of 'Our Missing Yeomen' could finally be published.

In his dispatch, published in September, General Murray, commander of the Egyptian Expeditionary Force, noted that, with the exception of sixty men and one officer, the squadrons

45. *An embroidered scarf sent to his family from India by Frederick Victor Summers. He enlisted in the Royal Garrison Artillery in November 1915, aged 18, and served in India. He later married Vera Brown (24). (Catherine and Peggy Guest)*

fell into the hands of the enemy and, 'I have therefore been able to gather no details of the actual fighting at Katia.' It did not help.

After the battle, the Worcestershire Yeomanry could only muster fifty-four men fit for duty and so the 2nd Australian Light Horse Brigade marched to the area the following day. They buried eighty Yeomen when they arrived and found another 300 bodies eight days later. Signaller J.C. Dorricott found the diary of Trooper George Pratt of Shenstone on the battlefield, and took the trouble to write to his parents offering to return it.

Local men were sent on a variety of postings to protect the British Empire, including India (45) where Captain Eustace Jotham, a native of Kidderminster, earned his Victoria Cross (Fact box 18). Another man with local connections, 2nd Lieutenant Edward Felix Baxter, earned a Victoria Cross on the Western Front (Fact box 19) where, by 1916, the more cautious John French had been replaced by the supremely confident and aloof Douglas Haig as commander of the British forces. The twenty-four divisions of Kitchener's armies of volunteers were equipped, trained and ready to fight – willing, but inexperienced. Measures to increase the output of guns, shells and other ammunition had first produced a sufficiency and then, by the middle of the year, the surplus needed to launch a major operation.

Offensives designed to break through the German lines and bring victory were planned. A French offensive in Verdun was thwarted when the Germans attacked first and so preparations were made for a joint offensive centred on the River Somme. The area behind the British lines was transformed into a vast army encampment of twenty divisions, with new roads leading to the front, over 1,400 gun emplacements and 3 million shells. These preparations were seen by the Germans, who interpreted them correctly and took their own defensive measures. Allied morale was high and optimistic of success.

Fact box 18

VC CITATION FOR EUSTACE JOTHAM, CAPTAIN, 51ST SIKHS, INDIAN ARMY
'For most conspicuous bravery on 7 January 1915 at Spina Khiasora (Tochi Valley) [on India's northwest frontier]. During operations against the Khostwal tribesmen, Captain Jotham, who was commanding a party of about a dozen of the North Waziristan Militia, was attacked in a nullah and almost surrounded by an overwhelming force of some 1,500 tribesmen. He gave the order to retire, and could have himself escaped, but most gallantly sacrificed his own life by attempting to effect the rescue of one of his men who had lost his horse.'

His name is on Kidderminster's war memorial.

A week-long bombardment of the German positions started on 24 June. However, it failed to cut most of the barbed wire entanglements that protected their trenches, did not reach the soldiers sheltering in dugouts 30ft below ground level, and did not clear the trenches or stun the surviving enemy into inactivity. On 1 July, in the expectation that all of these would have been achieved, 100,000 British infantry climbed out of their trenches and walked, upright, in daylight, across no-man's-land. They had only their cloth uniforms to protect them from the machine guns that the unscathed Germans brought out of their deep dugouts and set up with practised speed. If the British got as far as the barbed wire, along most of the front, it formed an impenetrable

Fact box 19

VC CITATION FOR EDWARD FELIX BAXTER, SECOND LIEUTENANT IN 1/8TH KING'S (LIVERPOOL) REGIMENT

'For most conspicuous bravery [on 18 April 1916]. Prior to a raid on the hostile line he was engaged during two nights in cutting wire close to the enemy's trenches. The enemy could be heard on the other side of the parapet.

Second Lieutenant Baxter, while assisting in the wire cutting, held a bomb in his hand with the pin withdrawn ready to throw. On one occasion the bomb slipped and fell to the ground, but he instantly picked it up, unscrewed the base plug, and took out the detonator, which he smothered in the ground, thereby preventing the alarm being given, and undoubtedly saving many casualties.

Later, he led the left storming party with the greatest gallantry, and was the first man into the trench, shooting the sentry with his revolver. He then assisted to bomb dugouts, and finally climbed out of the trench and assisted the last man over the parapet. After this he was not seen again, though search parties went out at once to look for him. There seems little doubt that he lost his life in his great devotion to duty.'

His name is on Kidderminster's war memorial.

barrier that turned them into sitting targets.

Captain E.A. Bland, of 22nd Manchester Regiment, whose parents lived at Greenhill, was killed by machine-gun fire whilst gallantly leading men exposed to 'an enfilading fire from both rifles and machine guns'. Just before the war he had been offered a professorship at Melbourne University, Australia. Private Fred W. Chance, aged 21, whose parents lived in Lea Street, a grenade bomber in the Manchesters, was also struck down. He had gone to work in Manchester at Easter, 1914. Bombardier Thomas Hall of Clensmore was wounded in the left thigh. He wrote from Southwark Military Hospital, 'When I got hit I had to leave everything behind, and have only got one or two things that I can call my own.' Pioneer C. Cecil Watkins, youngest son of Charles Watkins, ironmonger in the Horsefair and Oxford Street, was in the Signalling Section, Royal Engineers, and was wounded that day and sent to hospital in Bristol.

Only five divisions managed to reach the German trenches. Private J. Gilbert Harvey, secretary of Harvey's millers, was recommended for the Military Medal because 'On July 1 he showed devotion to duty and gallantry when a raid on the German trenches was made.'

46. *The discharge paper of Albert Henry Watkins as medically unfit, dated 8 May 1916, before the Somme offensive. It is signed by E.V.V. Wheeler. (Bob and Phill Millward)*

Once there ceased to be any risk to their own lives, the Germans stopped firing to allow the British walking wounded to return to their lines. In all, 20,000 men did not return from this first advance and another 40,000 returned wounded (46). The Germans lost about 6,000 killed and wounded.

The battalions of the Worcestershire Regiment were held in reserve on that first day but the 2/7th Worcesters (available for France once conscription was introduced) were in action shortly after. Private Albert Fosbrooke of Back Queen Street, an employee of Austin Brothers, coal merchants in Station Yard, was wounded in action on 5 July while raiding German trenches.

Captain Geoffrey Tomkinson was seriously wounded and sent to hospital in England. He had returned from Brazil to join the forces at the outbreak of war. Private Albert Hinett of Queen Street, an employee at Bateman's Sawmills, was buried in the debris thrown up by a bursting shell. He was unconscious when taken to the field hospital and suffered from shock. Corporal Cleon Francis Slater of Marlpool Lane, an employee of Tomkinson's, who had married Miss J. Pressland of Swan Street less than a year previously, died on 9 July. His lieutenant explained what happened:

47. *The officers of 1/7th Worcesters, photographed at Maldon.*

Back row: 2/Lt D.B. Drake, 2/Lt W.R. Prescott, Lt Homfray, 2/Lt J.G. Dixon. Second row: 2/Lt G.S. Tomkinson, Lt A.G. Rollason, Lt R.A. Leighton*, 2/Lt A.G. Gwilliam, Capt. N.P. Goodwin, Capt. F.D. Chamberlin, 2/Lt R. Armstrong, Capt. F.M. Tomkinson. Sitting: Capt. E.F. Dusautoy, Capt. & Adj. G. Davidge, Rev. P.C. Thomas, Lt/Col A.R. Harman, Major A.S.W. Dore, Major B. Addenbrooke (RAM.), Capt. W. Adam. Seated on ground: 2/Lt G.G. Watson, 2/Lt F.D.H. Burcher, Lt R.G. Addenbrooke, 2/Lt H.G.W. Wood. (Kidderminster Shuttle)

* Lt R.A. Leighton was the fiancé of Vera Brittain, author of Testament of Youth. *He joined the battalion in Maldon in March 1915 and died of wounds received nine months later.*

The Germans were firing aerial torpedoes across to our trenches, and up till then they had all fallen behind us. The men were all in firebays under shelter as far as possible, when a torpedo dropped on the back wall of the trench your husband was in and exploded. A fragment pierced his shrapnel helmet and entered his brain, and he died the same evening although removed to hospital at once.

In mid-July the 3rd and 1/7th Worcesters (47) moved into action against the village of Ovillers, just over 3 miles north-east of Albert, occupied by the Germans and the focus of continuous fighting since the start of the Somme offensive. Under the command of Lieutenant Colonel Davidge, adjutant at the Shrubbery before the war, 3rd Worcesters captured a German trench junction which, in effect, isolated the force in Ovillers and brought about its eventual surrender. However, on 13 July, before it was finally taken he was wounded. Lance Corporal H. Moses of 1/7th Worcesters, whose parents lived in East Street, described what happened in the following days:

We took the village of Ovillers with a rush [on 16 July], hand to hand fighting being carried on extensively. We then drove the enemy back to his third line. We took the fourth on the 18th, and started on the 5 on the 19th. I was just getting into their trench when I was hit. I managed to get back to the dressing station somehow.

He was wounded by shrapnel in the left knee and lost all his kit and personal belongings.

Private Jack Barlow, an employee of Tomkinson's, and a stretcher bearer with the 1/7th Worcesters, was wounded on 17 July in the left arm and leg by a shell and was sent to a hospital near Birmingham. The following day, his birthday, Private Thomas Packwood, who also worked for Tomkinson's, was wounded and wrote from hospital to his wife in Albert Road:

48. *Private F.G. Cooper of 1/7th Worcesters, who died 19 July 1916 at Ovillers, during the Somme offensive. He was 38. His last leave home had been Christmas 1915. He had worked at Brinton's, in the Axminster department, since he was a youth, and had been shop secretary for over two years. (Shirley Morgan)*

We had got all the German trenches except the last line when I got hit. We had about six lines of trenches all told, and the night I got hit our chaps went over but got badly cut up by machine guns. I felt sorry for those poor devils of Germans we captured, they gave themselves up in dozens but there was hardly one of them who hadn't got a wound of some sort from the terrible shelling our guns had given them ... they were in a pitiable state, and they told us they had not had a drop of water for five days. I had a lot of souvenirs such as helmets, buttons and revolvers, but when you get hit it takes you all of your time to get out of the danger zone.

A night attack on the 18/19 July, saw the deaths of sixteen men from the Kidderminster area, the highest number for one day recorded by the *Shuttle*. They included Private Frederick G. Cooper, 1/7th Worcesters, killed in action. His widow and five children lived in Hemming Street, and his mother in Wood Street (48)(49). Private Francis Hugh Burry, aged 21, whose father ran a fried fish shop in Blackwell Street, died from wounds received in action. The 19-year-old Private Victor Eaborn of the 1/7th Worcesters, who had been employed by Meredith Brothers and whose father lived in Clarence Street, was wounded in action and was sent to a hospital in Birmingham with shrapnel in both thighs and his left forearm.

Another notable death before the end of the month was Captain Charles Leslie Butcher, killed in France on 24 July, who was a director of Lea Ltd. Like many of the men who died in the Somme offensive he enlisted with the Worcesters at the outbreak of war. Before going to France his engagement to Miss

Borough of Kidderminster.

In Glorious Memory

of Pte. F.G. Cooper

who gave his life for his KING & COUNTRY
in the GREAT WAR.

Mayor

Town Clerk.

Elsie Goodwin, daughter of the proprietor of Goodwin & Co., millers, had been announced.

The Somme offensive, in the form of numerous hard-fought actions like that at Ovillers, made gains but not the major breakthrough that had been so confidently expected, and continued until November. Thiepval, an objective for the first day, was taken in the last month of the battle. By then the Allies had suffered 630,000 casualties and the Germans about 660,000.

It was not always easy for families to find out what had happened to those in the forces. Conditions on the front line were not conducive to good record keeping (Profile 5).

Conscription exacerbated another problem. In March 1916, William Moulder of Hoobrook, a conscript, was charged with being a deserter from the army. This was the second time he had left his regiment. He was remanded to await military escort. In April, Alfred Skerrett was arrested as a deserter at his home in

49. Commemorative certificate given to the family of Private F.G. Cooper by the Town Council. He left a widow and five children in Hemming Street. His mother lived in Wood Street. (Shirley Morgan)

R.S. Amos, Finding out the Fate of Loved Ones

Reginald Sidney Amos was born in Hall Street, one of thirteen children. By late 1915 he was in Smethwick with his family, having volunteered to do war work wherever needed. After attesting (20) Reginald was called up in January 1916, aged 21. He joined 10th Worcesters.

In 1917, when his family had not received a letter from him for some time, they enquired after Reginald. On 13 March the Infantry Record Office at Warwick sent a reply, which said that Lance Corporal R.S. Amos was still serving with his corps in France (pictured), and a letter stating that Private S.R. Amos was posted as missing on 11 February 1917 (pictured). They were the same man.

In June 1917 E. Batchelor, wrote from Hospital in Norfolk:

I only joined the 10th Worcs the night [of] the Bombing raid in which your brother was lost so I did not know him … They were unable to go out after the raid to find out who were missing but we went back into the same lines about a week after … so Sgt Carrol and a party went out in the morning and found some of the bodies and I understood at the time they found your brother but if Sgt Carrol wrote and told you they did not I misunderstood him. I am sorry to say Sgt Carrol is killed. … Our Commandant had a letter this a.m. about your brother from our C.O. for me to give information but I was unable to give any. I'm awfully sorry … I think we lost about 60 men that night your brother was missing …'

Reginald's last letter, dated January 1917, was forwarded to his family on 31 December.

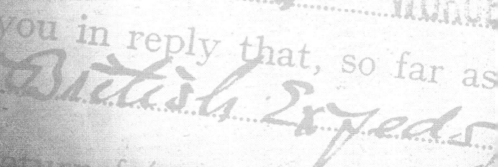

WORCESTERSHIRE REGT.

No. 11099
(If replying, please quote above No.)

Army Form B. 104—85.

Record Office,

_____ Station.

[stamp: INFANTRY RECORD OFFICE 13 MAR. 1917 WARWICK]

_____ 191

Madam

I have to acknowledge the receipt of your enquiry of the recent date
instant, regarding (No.) 39911 (Rank) Lce Corpl
Name R. S. Amos
Regiment 10th Batt. WORCESTERSHIRE REGT.
and to inform you in reply that, so far as is known, he is still serving
with his corps at British Expedy Force France

The latest return from the corps, on which the present information
is based, is dated 1st _____ 191

As all casualties to soldiers (including wounds and dangerous illness)
are reported home by cable, as far as possible, immediately after their
occurrence, and as no such information has been received in this office in
regard to the above-named soldier, it may be assumed that there are no
special grounds for your apprehension on his behalf.

Should any information be received _____
to you.

Your _____

(K11220) Wt W2537—250,000—8/14. W. & Co.,
Forms
B. 104-85.

(Ruby Henderson)

No. _____
(If replying, please quote above No.)

Army Form B. 104—83.

Record Office,

[stamp: INFANTRY RECORD OFFICE 13 MAR. 1917 WARWICK]

_____ Station.

_____ 191

Sir or MADAM,

I regret to have to inform you that a report has been received from the
War Office to the effect that (No.) 39911 (Rank) Pte
(Name) Amos S. R.
(Regiment) WORCESTERSHIRE REGT.
was posted as "missing" on the 11/2/17.

The report that he is missing does not necessarily mean that he has been killed, as
he may be a prisoner of war or temporarily separated from his regiment.

Official reports that men are prisoners of war take some time to reach this country,
and if he has been captured by the enemy it is probable that unofficial news will reach
you first. In that case, I am to ask you to forward any letter received at once to this
Office, and it will be returned to you as soon as possible.

Should any further official information be received it will be at once communicated
to you.

I am,
Sir, or MADAM,
Your obedient Servant,

Eric Allen

Lieut. for Br. General.
Officer i/c Infantry Records.
No. 17 DISTRICT

Important.—Any change of address should be immediately notified to this office.

(4-27-1) W5490—735 /150,000 8/16 HWV(P1205/1) Forms/B.104—83/2.

Silver Street, and John Beattie Cooper, of a Canadian battalion, and also a deserter, was posing as a lieutenant of the Tyneside Scottish Regiment. From 1916, lists of 'absentees' with local addresses were regularly published with a request to help trace them. In June 1918, Mrs Watkins, whose husband had just been arrested as a deserter, accused Mrs Hancocks of giving him away, causing a disturbance in the Horsefair. These were among the 39,060 wartime deserters, most of whom absconded in Britain, unwilling to return to the fighting. Just over 300 were executed, although many more were sentenced to death.

By the end of 1916 Lloyd George was Prime Minister and Lord Derby was Secretary of State for War, replacing Lord Kitchener who was a casualty of the war. Commanders of the French and German forces also changed and this promised the alteration of tactics on all sides for 1917.

The Germans withdrew from the Somme salient to the heavily fortified Hindenburg Line. Initially interpreted as a successful outcome of the Somme offensive, in fact it shortened the German front line and released men to fight elsewhere. British, Canadian and Australian forces planned to attack at Arras and Vimy Ridge, just beyond the northern end of the Hindenburg Line, with the French attacking the Aisne heights beyond the southern end.

The bombardment at Arras started on 4 April 1917 followed by an attack on 9 April, Easter Monday. Lessons had been learned. The accuracy of firing and quality of ammunition had both improved, and the barbed wire was torn to shreds. A new gas shell used against German batteries reduced their effective-ness and the tunnels of pre-existing subterranean quarries were augmented and used to bring the infantry forward under cover. Their advance was then successfully co-ordinated with a creeping artillery barrage, and much of the ridge was taken for relatively few Allied casualties. Local man, Gunner F.E. Bayes of the Royal Garrison Artillery, wrote 'We are doing fine work and I think old Fritz will soon have had enough of it. He cannot stand our artillery fire.'

However, an intermission allowing Allied casualties to be replaced and troops to recover also gave German reserves time to stop the gap. Battle resumed on 23 April. The 1/8th and 1/7th Worcesters were to take Gillemont Farm on the crest of a spur overlooking the main Hindenburg Line. Private Leonard Whittall, a boot repairer at Saunders' in New Road, was wounded in the arm by shrapnel while moving forward in preparation for the attack. He wrote, 'It was a lucky thing I was not killed for the shell only dropped a few yards away.'

Two companies of 1/8th attacked at 3.45 a.m. on 24 April. As they were advancing, Private John Cleaver Bishop, whose father was a coachbuilder in Coventry Street, was hit and killed. He was 31, and had married Miss Matthews of Foley Park. The letter from his commanding officer said his body had not been recovered but that he hoped he would be found and given a proper burial.

The spur was cleared and 1/8th started to entrench. However, neighbouring high ground had not been taken and, as the light grew, they were fired on from three sides. They held their ground, but men fell rapidly. At 8.30 a.m. a counter-attack pressed up the valleys on either side of the spur and closed in on the farm. The survivors withdrew to their original positions under heavy fire – they had suffered twenty-three dead, sixty-nine injured and sixty-three missing.

A second attempt was made by 1/7th at 11.00 p.m. After a confused struggle in the darkness they took the farm and hurriedly entrenched. Corporal Lawrence **Parsons**, whose parents ran the Duke of Edinburgh **Inn**, Bromsgrove Street, was badly wounded during this night attack and died, close behind, in a field hospital. He had enlisted in August 1914, leaving a job at the Stour Vale Ironworks and had recently been training for promotion. It was the 25-year-old Sergeant Bernard W. Onslow, whose father was a greengrocer in Mill Street, who informed Parsons' parents of his death, adding that 'his many Kidderminster friends join in tendering their sympathy'.

At dawn a storm of fire heralded a counter-attack that was beaten off with difficulty. Sergeant **Frank**

50. *Lieutenant Colonel F.M. Tomkinson, commander of 1/7th Worcesters. (H. FitzM. Stacke)*

Morris, a carpet worker of Dudley Street, was killed by a shell; Private George Cooper, whose mother lived on Bewdley Hill, suffered a gunshot wound to his left leg; and Corporal Gilbert Pritchard, whose father was a plumber and decorator in Bewdley Road, was wounded in the shoulder. Pritchard was the company runner and was expecting promotion to commissioned officer rank. Altogether the Battalion suffered fourteen killed, ninety-four wounded and twenty-nine missing. Nevertheless, the position was held.

The 1/7th Battalion commander, Lieutenant Colonel F.M. Tomkinson, received a bar to his DSO (50), and the bravery of others on these two days was also recognised. Sergeant J.T. Sadler, of Prospect Lane, an employee of Baldwin's, was awarded the Military Medal for the engagement. The official particulars described how:

> He assisted his officer on all reconnaissances for forward positions, and then helped to get his guns forward in support of infantry. Later when his guns had been forced to retire owing to counter attack, he took them forward again under heavy barrage and after getting them into fresh positions, went forward to discover exact position of enemy.

They had advanced 5 miles, and Private C.W. Blencowe wrote: 'We have had a very busy time of late. All the reclaimed villages here are little more than heaps of ruins.' Gunner J. Preen, previously of Victoria Carpets, wrote optimistically to his mother in Albert Road, 'We are still keeping the Germans on the run and we are having grand weather.'

For the next month attrition set in, with numerous similar individual engagements. By the time the battle stopped the Allies had lost 150,000 men killed or wounded. Gerald W.G. Allbut, whose father was manager of the Co-op in Kidderminster, was dangerously wounded in the abdomen, and his parents were told that 'permission to visit him could not be granted'. He died from his wounds on 27 April and was buried at Peronne Military Cemetery. A German shell landed in the dugout of Walter Edwards of Wood Street,

51. *A Christmas card of 1916 showing a British 'Tommy' with a German prisoner of war. (Ruby Henderson)*

shattering both his legs, but he hoped to come through and go back to his old job as a horse driver in the council's Health Department.

The supporting French attack on the Aisne was delayed until 16 April. The Germans had obtained advance warning and strengthened their defences. The result was a catastrophic defeat for the French. Their high casualty rate led to mutinies in the French army, who would defend the trenches but not attack.

At Ypres an allied salient projected forward into the German lines, but this was not a point of weakness for the Germans. They occupied a ridge of higher ground which gave them an uninterrupted view and firing line over Allied positions and protected their own rear positions from easy observation. They had fortified their position with multiple lines of trenches, some in front of the ridge, forward listening posts, machine-gun posts and pillboxes.

A counter-attack zone to the rear sheltered most of their forces, to be used after their front line had halted an initial Allied assault.

Repeated shelling had cleared the land below the ridge of trees and buildings. It had also destroyed the stream banks and land drainage channels, creating a flat surface of deep, gluey mud. With most of the French Army incapacitated by mutinies, it was the British, with Canadian and Australian support, who had to take the lead in any Allied offensive action. The taking of Messines, the southern end of the ridge, in June 1917 convinced Haig that it was possible to take the rest of the ridge. The plan was to take bites out of the German positions, taking an objective, moving the artillery forward, and recommencing the process.

The Third Battle of Ypres commenced with an Allied attack at dawn on 31 July, after fifteen days of bombardment. Infantry and tanks made good progress, including 1st Worcesters. Two companies followed the creeping barrage and swept forward over the German front and support lines, capturing a tunnel under the road with forty German prisoners (51). They dug in and the other two companies passed through to Chateau Wood, capturing another trench. Machine-gun fire and shelling did not prevent them achieving their initial objectives and gaining a foothold on the ridge.

A German counter-attack in the afternoon followed by torrential rain slowed progress. The rain lasted for another three days and flooded parts of the battlefield. The Germans could concentrate shell fire on any attacking force struggling through the mud. Private Victor Denning, whose mother lived in Broad Street, was killed on the first day. Corporal A. Hill of Lancashire Fusiliers was mortally wounded and taken to a Belgian hospital. He had relatives in Park Lane and had worked in the dye house at R. Smith & Sons before enlisting in August 1914. He died on 3 August. Private C. Penson of Chester Road was injured by the bursting of a German shell near his dugout. Although he was hit in seventeen places most were small splinters and only those in his legs were serious.

As ever, officers suffered. Second Lieutenant Peter Adam, son of carpet magnate Peter Adam, 'fell at the head of his company while behaving in a most gallant manner under heavy shell fire, and was killed instantaneously'. Second Lieutenant R.E. Grove, in the local

Territorials before the war and commissioned in the Machine Gun
Corps, had recovered from a slight wound and returned to France
on 30 July only to be severely wounded three days later.

There was a remarkable feat of survival, too. Private
W.R. Sparry, conscripted into the Grenadier Guards, aged 19, had
worked for Thursfields before being called up. He was wounded
by machine-gun fire delivering a message to a lieutenant, who
was killed by the same gun. Sparry managed to crawl 4 miles
through the mud to a dressing station and just over a week later
he was in a Cardiff hospital.

By the time a temporary halt was called, on 4 August, the Allies
had suffered 35,000 casualties – killed, wounded and missing.

The Germans retained control of the higher ground, in spite
of continued attacks. There was sharp fighting at Langemarck in
August. Private G.E. Pryce of King's Royal Rifle Corps, whose
mother lived in Dudley Street, was killed 'almost instantaneously'
by a German shell. Private W.J. Jennings of 2/7th Worcesters,
whose parents lived in Hurcott Road, died less than a week after
returning to duty from hospital. He had enlisted in August 1914.
Private W. Cooper was wounded on 18 August when 'Old
Fritz started to shell us.' He was carried to the nearest dressing
station. Corporal Arthur Matthews, of 1/7th Worcesters, was
severely wounded in the lower jaw by a piece of shell. A letter
to his parents in St Mary's Street was written by Major Bertram
Addenbrooke, treating him at Rouen:

He came out to France with me, and I think he possibly
remembered me better than I remembered him. Eventually
I think he will completely recover. He is quite cheerful,
though it is distressing not to be able at the present time
to talk, and also the matter of feeding is not easy.

He was sent to England for specialist treatment.

The Allies managed to advance to the foot of Passchendaele
Ridge, a position vulnerable to fire from above. Therefore, Haig
decided to continue attacking the ridge in October. Allied shells
were burying themselves in the soft ground without exploding,

and barbed wire remained uncut so that casualties among the attacking British, ANZAC and Canadian divisions were heavy. Sergeant Charles Ingles, whose parents lived in Blackwell Street, was killed on 9 October, after two years in the army. He had previously worked at Naylor's. Private A.G. Rollings, whose parents lived in Wood Street, died in the same action. He had joined the 1/7th Worcesters after three rejections.

The target, the ruined Passchendaele village, was eventually taken on 6 November, bringing the entire ridge into Allied hands. It created a dangerous salient, but the rain made further advance impossible. There had been over 240,000 Allied casualties. The German casualties were also high and could no longer be fully replaced. The battle took the pressure off the French forces, giving them time to regain their fighting spirit. However, it exhausted the British, who had also had difficulty replacing their losses and so they lowered the medical threshold for their conscripts. Importantly, the Allies had found tactics that worked, even if they did not produce a quick decision.

In April 1917 the United States declared war, and their forces started arriving in France in June. The Americans did not have tanks, artillery or aircraft, but these were provided by the French. Potentially, the Americans were a vast additional source of manpower at a time when the British and French were finding it difficult to fill the gaps in their ranks. British conscripts were sent where they were needed and reorganisation of the army, to cope with the losses, had transferred men between regiments. By 1918, Kidderminster men were spread across many regiments (Fact box 20).

The political collapse of Russia in 1917 enabled the Germans to transfer fifty infantry divisions

Fact box 20

THE UNITS OF DECEASED SOLDIERS FROM KIDDERMINSTER AND DISTRICT, RECORDED IN THE KIDDERMINSTER SHUTTLE

	1915		1918	
Worcestershire Regiment	79	49%	44	24%
Worcestershire Yeomanry	3	2%	–	–
Royal Field Artillery	5	3%	19	10%
Other units	73	45%	119	64%
Died after Discharge	2	1%	5	2%
Total	162	100%	187	100%

to the Western Front. But they had no other replacements to call on. They needed to win the war before the Americans arrived, and before their attacking troops became exhausted. Food shortages, due to Allied blockade of German ports, had already weakened them. Speed was all important. Their offensive of 1918 was their last chance of victory. On 21 March they launched their attack along the St Quentin front with a five hour bombardment using explosive and gas shells. They overran a 12 mile stretch of front suffering heavy losses but inflicting defeat on the British, whose morale and cohesion were low. The British suffered 17,000 casualties, and 21,000 men were taken prisoner. However, German casualties totalled 39,000. A week later the British were fighting back. The Germans had advanced 20 miles, but their pace was slowed by the broken terrain. They also stopped to gorge themselves on the food and liquor they found in the British rear areas. A British and Australian counter-attack persuaded the Germans to halt the attack.

They launched four more offensives, each of which was quickly halted as casualties soared and defence stiffened. Superior tanks and American assistance were crucial to the Allies. The last German attack was halted on 18 July.

In August the Allies launched their own attacks against a demoralised German army. But German resistance stiffened as the army fell back and there were heavy casualties. Company Sergeant Major Phipps wrote in October 1918 about the big battle there had been with heavy casualties and hoping the Germans were now 'on the run'. The guns were going from morn till night. One soldier had not had his boots off for seven weeks. Having finally broken German lines soldiers were exhausted by the swift advance.

The other central powers sued for peace. Bulgaria, Turkey and Austria all withdrew from the war leaving Germany isolated. Elsewhere, Germany's fleet mutinied and Berlin was in political turmoil as the Bolsheviks unsuccessfully tried to take power. An armistice delegation of military and civil personnel made contact with the French. The Kaiser departed for Holland, leaving Germany effectively a republic, and the Armistice was signed, coming into effect on 11 November 1918, just before the total exhaustion of the Allies.

5

LIFE AT HOME

The Aliens' Restriction Act of 5 August 1914, the day after Britain declared war, allowed the government to intern enemy aliens, although the power was not used until May 1915. Hostility towards aliens was strong. Frederick Bauer, whose German father was interned, was a gut scraper for sausage skins at the Old Pencil Factory in Coventry Street. The council's sanitary inspector had to be subpoenaed to appear at the tribunal on

52. *Notice published by John Sneader in February 1916. He was a Jew, born in Birmingham.* (Kidderminster Shuttle)

PUBLIC NOTICE.

The undersigned, J. SNEADER, Jeweller and Watchmaker, of 20, Oxford Street, hereby informs the Public of Kidderminster that he is a British Subject, born in England, and that Legal Proceedings will be taken against any person stating the contrary.

J. SNEADER.

**20, OXFORD STREET,
KIDDERMINSTER.**   7622

his behalf. The Butchers' Association asserted that gut scraping was a necessary trade for the public food supply and there was a prohibition on importing sausage skins. After an appeal he was exempted from military service.

John Sneader, a Jewish jeweller in Oxford Street, was suspected of being a German and asserted his nationality in the local paper (52). When he was examined at the tribunal, Tomkinson commented that there was 'more honour in being a Jew than a German', which subsequent history has imbued with greater meaning than its speaker intended.

In February 1915 the Civilian Rifle Association became the Volunteer Training Corps. Their first drill station was Cooke Brothers' warehouse at Worcester Cross. They expected to move to the Shrubbery once the forces recruited to serve abroad had left the town. The Volunteers were recognised as a military force for home defence. Members took the oath of allegiance and received military rank and status. The 150 strong Kidderminster Company commanded by W.H. Stewart-Smith with R.S. Brinton as a platoon commander, was part of the 1st Worcestershire Volunteer Battalion.

They received no government grants so uniforms, equipment and weapons had to be provided by the members. By June 1915 the Kidderminster Company all had uniforms but needed help to meet their remaining costs. The council resisted requests for assistance until 1916 when the honorary secretary requested a grant to clear a £16 debt and buy more equipment. The council could not legally make a grant, but they increased the mayor's salary by £50 to be passed on to the corps. There was laughter at this sleight of hand.

In May 1916 the military tribunal resolved that men exempted from service should be urged to join the Volunteers or the Special Constables. Later this was made compulsory (21). Initially it was not taken seriously, so withdrawal of exemptions was threatened and requests to be excused were often dismissed. Henry Cowderoy, commercial traveller of Stourport Road, submitted a doctor's certificate to support his claim that he was unable to join the Volunteers, but was ordered to drill with them every other Sunday.

The Volunteer Regulations required a man to do ten hours drilling a month. The company did drills every Sunday, and also had shooting practice, route marches and ambulance drills. Training camps and exercises were held on bank holidays. The men had to provide their own equipment and a sack filled with straw for sleeping. In August 1915 the Kidderminster Company marched to a training camp at Hagley Park, led by the Kidderminster Brigade Band and accompanied by another forty people. The public paid 3*d* towards battalion funds for admission to the camp.

In August 1914 local authorities were empowered to appoint special constables to augment the police. Kidderminster's Special Constables were established on 1 May 1915 with 120 men, all unpaid. Eight men, working in pairs, were on duty each night. They were also commanded by W.H. Stewart-Smith, with R.S. Brinton as a section commander. One of the sergeants was W.H. Taylor (Profile 6).

They assisted with lighting controls, implemented against the possibility of night bombing raids by German Zeppelins, which had started in January 1915. The signal to warn of the approach of a Zeppelin was four short blasts on the 'Brinton's Bull' followed by one long blast (3). All gas and electricity would be turned off at the mains and remain off for the rest of the night. Residents were warned against rushing into the streets, reminded that cellars and basements were the safest places, and told not to fire at any hostile aircraft.

The government suggested that hospitals should conspicuously position a large panel, divided into black and white portions, so that they would be recognised in the event of a bombardment or hostile landing. Alderman Tomkinson did not think the 'satellites of the butcher of Potsdam' would take any notice. Rev. A Gibson claimed the Germans had 'out-Heroded Herod' by bombing undefended towns.

These precautions were justified when, on the 31 January 1916, two Zeppelins appeared just over the county border in Staffordshire and dropped forty-five bombs. At least one of the Zeppelins passed over Kidderminster, but all lights in the town had been extinguished and it was not attacked. (It is thought an unexploded bomb, discovered below river level in 1939 whilst rebuilding the Worcester Road Bridge, was dropped during this raid.) When, ten days later, there was a false alarm, at the sound of Brinton's Bull 'the populace ran with their usual haste to see the fire, a haste a little exceeded on the return home when they heard the real cause of the alarm'. Batches of bread were left unbaked, theatres and cinemas were emptied, and scores of people spent the night in their cellars. At the Opera House the band continued playing until everyone had left, and the evacuated patrons were invited to return free the following night.

These events galvanised local institutions to take out 'aircraft insurance' against damage from enemy aircraft or anti-aircraft action. St Mary's Church was insured for £28, and an air raid insurance scheme for households was made available through the Post Office.

In April 1916, the government prohibited the striking of church clocks and the ringing of bells at night, so that they could be used as warnings.

The major defence against being bombed at night was total darkness. Under Defence of the Realm legislation, authorities were given the power to demand lights be extinguished (Fact box 21). Initially people were reluctant, but after the arrival of the Zeppelin the threat was taken more seriously. People wore luminous buttons so that they could be seen when they went out after dark. Fines of between 5s and 20s were imposed where lights were shown after restricted lighting time: Joseph Bristow did not have the lights protected at the Duke of York Club on Arch Hill; Annie Moule allowed a bright light to be seen from the concert room of the Roebuck Inn (7); Caroline Chivers of Cobden Street had a candle in the bedroom with no blind to the window; and Elsie Hubble of Park Street, who had a bright light in the kitchen with only a white blind, was one of many who did not realise that the back premises also had to be protected. An exasperated chief constable wished that people would understand that the back was as important as the front.

WILLIAM HENRY TAYLOR, SPECIAL CONSTABLE

William Henry Taylor and Jane Bell married in May 1893, when they were both aged 22. William purchased adjacent properties in Chester Road, one to live in and one to let, and used the outbuildings for his business ventures.

As an agent for Calder's Yeast Co. he had a staff of men delivering the yeast to farmers. When they enlisted, William's sister and daughter, Julia and Florence, took over the deliveries. They loaded their bicycles, caught the train to Bridgnorth and cycled home delivering the yeast en route.

William built a sugar-boiling workshop and sold the sweets he made from his stall in Market Hall.

As a prosperous businessman he was elected to the town council in 1914.

At the outbreak of war William was over the age limit for armed service. Instead, he was one of six sergeants in the town's special constables. The picture shows him in uniform making sure his badge of office recording 'Special Constable 50' is clearly visible to the camera; his pride is evident. He and his colleagues undertook the inspection of the national registration cards of all men between 15 and 65 years old in July 1916. The town council thanked them for the courteous and energetic way they had carried out these duties. Mr Taylor, in his capacities as councillor and special constable, thanked the council. At the end of the war he received a certificate of appreciation signed by the chief constable of the borough, Frederick Gray.

In 1920, after the death of William's brother-in-law, Samuel Frederick Bell, his widow, Laura Bell, came to live with them.

William's business activities were lucrative. In 1922, he commissioned the building of a bungalow in Chester Road for the sum of £1,099 4s 9d.

(Nicky Griffiths)

53. *Notice published
in October 1916
curtailing
deliveries due to
restricted lighting.*
(Kidderminster
Shuttle)

Where lighting regulations were broken in the houses of the middle and upper classes it was the servants who were sent before the magistrate. Annie Crowe, a maid at the residence of R.S. Brinton, was fined 5s. His wife said she had told the maids not to use the lighted room until a blind was fitted.

The reading room at the Free Library was closed at sunset to avoid the expense of covering the lantern roof, until blinds were fitted in October 1916.

In order to make the most of the daylight a 'Daylight Savings Act' came into operation on 21 May 1916, when every clock in the country was advanced one hour beyond Greenwich Mean Time. 'Summer time' was intended to save the nation £2,500,000 in lighting and fuel.

Alongside the lighting restrictions was a requirement for all vehicles to have lights to make them visible in the darkness, white at the front and red at the rear. The first prosecution was in March 1916. Reginald Lloyd aged 10, Kitty Hopkins aged 11 and George Williams aged 13, were sent out with wheelbarrows for coal late at night without any lights. The case was a warning to the public and there were no fines. The regulations applied to all vehicles, including an army tank, which travelled through Kidderminster twice on the night of 13 September 1917. It was accompanied on its journey by men carrying lanterns.

Shops and churches tried to cope as best they could. Grocer, C.W. Clarke curtailed deliveries (53), Findon's Grocery Stores shut earlier during the winter months in order to complete deliveries before dark, and places of worship altered the time of their evening services.

The departure of men to fight created serious problems for commerce, and some businesses were forced to close. In April 1916 'the entire capital, and builders' and general ironmongery stock' of Pheysey Ltd, ironmonger in Vicar Street, was sold at short notice, 'owing to enlistment of staff' (54). Ye Old Swan Temperance Hotel in Swan Street also closed; it had served commercial travellers, motorists, cyclists and tourists, all categories of client that had been substantially reduced by the war.

Many men risked losing their livelihood. In January 1916 the borough tribunal told Rowland Onslow, fruiterer, to get rid of his business. Other businesses, such as shoe makers and repairers, depended solely on their personal skill. Albert Taylor, in Marlborough Street, had been fifteen years working up his present clientele and his business would fold without him.

Numerous employees enlisted, and all the staff at Roberts & Co. clothiers shop in Oxford Street joined the forces. John Henry Brain, house decorator, builder and plumber in Coventry Street, had only sixteen men at work in May 1916, compared to his

54 *The sale of Pheysey's Ironmongers at 5 Vicar Street, in April 1916.* (Kidderminster Shuttle)

normal twenty-five to thirty. Meredith Brothers, grocers in High Street, lost twenty-six employees.

The army's desperation for men in 1917 is clearly seen in the increasingly crass and cruel comments made by J.T. Pilling about men appearing before the tribunal. When B. Waldron, a baker in Stourport Road, applied for exemption claiming he was only 4ft 11in tall, Pilling at once observed, 'a useful man in a tank'. George Grimley, aged 41, of Mill Street, had a furniture shop in Park Butts, and Pilling asked him if he thought the dressing of his shop window was more important than beating the Germans.

The loss of manpower had a serious effect on many of Kidderminster's businesses. In a letter of 1917, H.G. Ivens, solicitor, wrote, 'I am myself overworked beyond all bounds, my office having been emptied of clerks and I having to do everything myself except what a lady stenographer can do.'

Employers wanted to keep the staff they had trained, so they tried to employ people unlikely to be conscripted into the army: Harvey's, the wine merchants, wanted a youth or man 'outside military age' for their warehouse and deliveries; William Thomas Hodges, gilder and picture frame maker in Oxford Street, wanted an ineligible man who was experienced in the trade. The biggest non-military group available was women, and employers increasingly looked to them to fill the gaps in their staff. Simpson & Son, fishmongers, advertised for a 'Lady Clerk' to take charge of their office, and by April 1916 the Tramway Company was getting desperate, advertising for 'men and women for spare time tram driving and conducting' (see Profile 4). As the school leaving age was lowered for those who had reached an appropriate level of attainment, there were adverts aimed at these young potential employees. E. Rollings, newsagent in Oxford Street, wanted to employ, full-time, a boy or girl aged 13 or 14.

Later in the war some businessmen looked to employ discharged soldiers and, in September 1916, Meredith Brothers advertised for two men for warehouse and stables, 'discharged soldiers preferred'. It became almost impossible to get skilled or experienced men, and Horace Green, a skilled plumber and fitter, worked seventy to eighty hours a week to satisfy demnd.

Eventually the government decided that substitution would help employers release any remaining fit men for military service. Men, whose level of fitness or domestic responsibilities prevented them from joining the army, were ordered to be substitutes for fit young men in certified occupations who could then join the forces. In July 1917 Rowland H. Minett, aged 40, a tobacconist in Blackwell Street, became a substitute at the British Tool & Engineering Co. in Wolverhampton, who duly released a man from the top fitness grade for the army. As the shortage of men at home became more acute, any that were exempt from the armed forces were ordered to do work of 'national importance' whether it released a man for the front or not. F. Pratt of Lickhill Farm, Stourport, agreed to employ Henry T. Davis, gentleman's outfitter in Swan Street, for two days a week on his farm. Albert Pugh, coal dealer and draper in Peel Street, obtained work for two days a week on a farm in Park Lane – shortages probably meant that he had the time to spare from his own business.

In May 1917 a National Service Scheme office was opened in the Town Hall for the substitution of volunteers in 'work of national importance'. The tribunal ordered the less fit men, aged 45–50 years old, to register.

As jobs for women increased with regular wages and fixed, albeit long, hours, a servant's life became much less attractive and large numbers left to work elsewhere. Sarah Jenkins' servants' registry in Mill Street closed in early 1916. Local adverts for Bird's Custard embodied this change (55).

Nevertheless, after its initial collapse in 1914, the town's economy revived as it adjusted to wartime conditions. In 1915 and 1916 food and drink were still in good supply, the market flourished, and munitions workers earned and spent good money. John Sneader, a jeweller in Oxford Street, reported that he was very busy, to which the mayor responded, 'supplying munition workers I expect'. People were investing in gold. The Gas Company opened a new showroom in the Bull Ring in May 1916, and urged its customers to consider turning to gas stoves for the winter as coal was becoming 'a scarce and dear commodity'.

Reduced supplies and some shortages, alongside higher wages, increased munitions employment and separation allowances for the women, inevitably led to inflation. In June 1915 the Kidderminster Gas Company increased the price of gas by 6d per 1,000 cubic feet. The company also supplied coke, but the shortage of men and horses created difficulty with deliveries. In September the price of electricity was increased by 10 per cent for power purposes and 12.5 per cent for lighting purposes.

Petrol too, was in short supply and its use for excursions and pleasure trips was prohibited from the beginning of September 1916. It could still be used for the conveyance of wounded soldiers, munitions workers, and work associated with hospital, naval, military and munitions services. By the end of June 1916 a pre-war wage of £2 a week was worth only 26s, representing inflation of 54 per cent since the start of the war. By May 1918 the prices of food, rent, lighting, coal and clothing had almost doubled since July 1914 and the £2 wage was only worth 20s 6d.

55. These adverts for Bird's Custard were published in August 1915 and August 1916. In twelve months, the focus had changed from families with servants to busy working women. (Kidderminster Shuttle)

War bonuses, which would continue until three months after the end of the war, were intended to counter the effects of inflation on employees' wages. Many workers for the local authority were awarded war bonuses of 2s per week, and the police were granted a war bonus of 2s 6d each. As wages improved, especially for women, dependence on credit reduced. The Co-op (6) was a

major beneficiary, with more women able to take advantage of their lower prices and receive the dividend. Sales for the year to March 1916 totalled £92,207, up by £14,940 over the previous year. A year later, membership went up by 286 to 3,321 and over £9,000 was paid out in dividends.

Smaller businesses were badly affected by the war. The government issued an appeal suggesting that people continue to patronise those shops whose owners or assistants had joined the military, and not transfer their patronage to other establishments (56). Reduced opening hours were agreed, probably as a consequence of labour shortages: in March 1916 shop assistants' hours were limited to sixty-five per week and in August all shops in the borough, except fish fryers and tripe dressers, were required to close by 9.00 p.m. Fridays, 10.00 p.m. Saturdays and 8.00 p.m. the rest of the week.

In 1915 the Parliamentary War Savings Committee explained the necessity of economy – the government needed over £1,000 million per annum to pay for the war, but had revenue of only about a quarter of this amount. The shortfall could only be partly met by taxation which was increased to five shillings in the pound. There was a need to buy less at home and sell more abroad. This could be done by saving, travelling less and producing more food at home.

In 1916 the government introduced a scheme of regular saving for the war effort, in an attempt to take advantage of the prosperity evident in many towns. In June the local council established the Kidderminster War Savings Association, with the assertion that the more money that was saved the quicker the war would end. Its President was R.S. Brinton, with E. George Eddy as its honorary financial secretary.

Support Those who Fight.

The Mayor has received the following letter from Whitehall, copies of which may be obtained at the Town Hall for display in the windows of shops and other establishments on behalf of which the appeal is made :—

Whitehall, S.W., July 20th.

Dear Sir,—The development of recruiting in recent months and the passing of the Military Service Acts have led to a large number of men joining the colours, whose absence from their ordinary avocations cannot but result in some dislocation of their businesses.

We feel sure that it is the universal desire that the men who are going forth to fight our country's battles shall in their civil positions suffer as little as possible for their patriotism, and we wish to appeal to the public to help to secure this object by continuing to support the shops and businesses of men who have themselves or whose assistants have joined the King's forces and by avoiding during the war the transfer of their patronage to other establishments.

May we ask you to let this appeal be circulated in your city, borough, or district

We are, dear Sir, yours faithfully,
HERBERT SAMUEL,
Home Secretary.
L. HARCOURT,
Acting President Board of Trade.
WALTER H. LONG,
President Local Government Board.
The Mayor of Kidderminster.

56. *An appeal to the public to continue supporting shopkeepers and small traders.* (Kidderminster Shuttle)

The minimum subscription was 6*d* per week, with savers receiving a War Savings Certificate when their subscriptions reached 15*s* 6*d*. After five years each certificate would be worth £1, a yield of 5.25 per cent, free of income tax. Factories, societies, schools and other communities were encouraged to form associations affiliated to this. Employers were urged to organise their workers under the scheme. Fifteen associations were formed in Kidderminster in its first month of operation (Fact box 22).

In mid-July, a War Savings Week was inaugurated as, 'a national self-denial week when the government desire that the clergy of all denominations should preach sermons on thrift and economy'. This prompted many companies to start associations. The War Savings Journal noted that, 'both large and small towns did well in war savings week … Kidderminster stands out with £1,000' and the National Committee expressed their delight at Kidderminster's achievement. By mid-August, about £200 per week was being saved at Brinton's, with up to 80 per cent of employees investing. Some workplace associations had over 120 members.

Kidderminster schools adopted a 'penny a week' scheme. New Meeting School invested 5,000 pennies in its first three weeks. In September the *Shuttle* stated, 'The town has reason to be proud of the results so far attained, seeing that it is not in the munition area.' It did not want to draw enemy attention (or Zeppelins) to the reason for its wealth. Alongside these investments, a Victory War Loan

---

Fact box 22

WAR SAVINGS IN KIDDERMINSTER

	Investment to Date	Number of Affiliated Associations
1916		
July	£1,000	25
August	–	30
September	£14,000	–
1917		
June	£54,146	–
September	£59,159	42
1918 (all savings, including loans, bonds, special investment weeks*)		
February	£376,829	–
July	£900,000	–
October	£1,000,000	56

*Including:

Victory War Loan 1917	£257,428
National War Bonds 1917/18	£61,785
Tank Bank Week 1918	£188,000
Businessman's Week 1918	£71,448
War Weapons Week 1918	£64,417

raised £257,428 by the beginning of February 1917 and investors loaned their earlier purchases of gold at the Post Office.

In one February week the town invested £1,786 5s in war savings certificates, representing an investment of 1s–2s per head of population, although investors also came from Kidderminster's hinterland. After this, weekly savings declined from £835 in March to just over £300 in June, although nearly 70,000 certificates had been purchased. Encouragement was needed. Streamers were displayed in High Street and Vicar Street bearing such slogans as 'Hasten Victory Buy 15s 6d Certificates'.

In November, National War Bonds were launched paying 5 per cent interest. During the first week of December £5,230 was subscribed locally, about 4s 4d per head of population, a remarkable total given the town's recent efforts. In the first twenty weeks Kidderminster people invested £61,785, an average of 2s 6d per person per week. Adverts encouraged people to draw out their savings and put them into war bonds (57).

FIRE

your Money at the Huns

JOIN the multitude of patriotic investors who all this week have been hurrying to lend their money to their country. Draw out your savings and buy War Bonds. Back up our lads at the Front with the full strength of your bank balance. Help to win our Gun.

THE GUN that will speak for Kidderminster

Don't delay. Every tick of your watch brings you nearer to the end of the week, nearer to the end of this great opportunity. Go to the Bank or Money Order Post Office and invest every shilling you possibly can. No sum can be too large. But do not think your help is not required even if you have only a few shillings to invest. Those few shillings may pay for the explosive that sends the first shell hurtling forth from our own Gun.

Buy **National War Bonds**

and War Savings Certificates

57. *An invitation to buy National War Bonds and War Savings Certificates in July 1918.* (Kidderminster Shuttle)

In 'Tank Bank Week', 14 April 1918, a tank, weighing 27 tons and measuring 30ft long, was to arrive at the station, negotiate a few obstacles on its way into town, and stand near the Rowland Hill statue for the week. On Sunday, the mayor, local dignitaries and Kidderminster Military Band headed a parade to the station to meet the tank. Cheers rang out as it rumbled out of the station and began its descent of Station Hill. It reached an obstruction of sandbags and wire which had been put across the road and slowly climbed up the pile and descended the other side. It was cheered for clearing the obstacle, and then it stopped and could not be moved (58). Pins in the caterpillar treads had broken. The tank was guarded at night by the local Volunteers with rifles and fixed bayonets, and Station Hill was blocked to traffic until Thursday when the tank was repaired and finally driven into town. £188,000 was raised, between £7 and £8 per head.

Other special weeks were equally successful. 'Businessman's Week' raised £71,448. 'War Weapons Week', in July 1918, aimed to raise £50,000 for three 12in howitzers, to be known as the 'Kidderminster Guns'. It was promoted by a display of weapons captured on the Somme in Attwood's shop window, and streamers across the street.

In October 1918 investments in the war effort by Kidderminster people reached the landmark of £1 million. A letter from the National War Savings Committee congratulated everyone on their contribution towards winning the war. In all, 6,000 people had invested in War Bonds and War Savings Certificates each week.

58. The tank which blocked Station Hill for several days in July 1918. (Kidderminster Library)

Unfortunately, the drinks industry was not able to benefit from this increased prosperity because legal measures to reduce drunkenness were introduced in August 1914, and expanded thereafter, 'for the purpose of increasing the efficiency of labour and preventing [it] from being impaired by drunkenness, alcoholism or excess'. Liquor Control Regulations enabled the government to control where, when and how much liquor was sold. They were specifically applied to Kidderminster. In August 1916, beer production was reduced by 15 per cent and the licensing of new breweries was forbidden. Prices quickly increased, and in April 1916 the Worcester, Kidderminster and District Bottlers' Association announced a price increase that included bottles of Guinness rising to 2s 6d per dozen. Two weeks later, they were increased by another 2d per dozen.

In March 1916 all licensed premises were placed out of bounds to soldiers between 6.00 a.m. and 12 noon, unless the soldiers had slept there the previous night. By 1916, all pubs in Kidderminster closed at 9.30 p.m. In February 1918, the landlord of the Black Horse was charged with serving alcohol out of hours, although the pub staff claimed that the drinks were theirs. The special constables interviewing them were told by the pub's charlady, 'Fancy you four men being here while my husband is in the trenches. You ought to be in the trenches.' The 'No Beer' sign was hoisted in the windows of several pubs during the last week of June 1917. By then, the permitted output of beer had been reduced to one third of the amount brewed in 1916. It was not drunkenness that these measures addressed but the need to produce grain for food. In October 1917, after a good harvest, the amount which could be brewed was increased by 20 per cent, although the alcohol content was limited and maximum prices of 4d or 5d per pint were specified to control inflation.

Imports of food from enemy countries stopped. Ships were seconded to the war effort, and many were destroyed by German U-boats leading to significant reductions – wheat imports declined by at least 15 per cent. Pre-war food levels did not only need to be maintained, they needed to be increased. Soldiers on active service required about 4,000 calories a day, much more than many had eaten in peacetime. Exhortations were made to grow more food, and to eat less bread and meat. After conscription was introduced in January 1916 most remaining farm workers were exempted. In July the Board of Agriculture specified that farms should have one man per 50 acres of land, but some farmhands were given exemptions in order to help with the harvest.

In January 1917, an addition to the Defence of the Realm Regulations empowered the Board of Agriculture and Fisheries to require an occupier of land to cultivate it in a manner designed to maintain the food supply of the country. The following month it was invoked in Kidderminster, when the tribunal threatened to withdraw Francis Higley's conditional exemption because some land on Halifax Farm in Franche was out of cultivation (59). The lack of farm labour was so acute that in June 1916 the government decided that any soldiers who were in England could work on farms. In August the Army Council placed 27,000 soldiers at the disposal of agriculturists for harvest work, allotting 225 to the Kidderminster district.

All hands were needed, including children. The Board of Guardians decided that the eleven boys in the children's home should continue their instruction in gardening instead of joining the Boy Scouts. In September 1916 many children went hop-picking and potato-digging, leading to 1,822 absences from school. In 1918 Kidderminster's Boy Scouts were recruited to collect any household refuse suitable for feeding to pigs, as it was feared their feeding stuff would soon run out.

59. Halifax Farm: in July 1916 Francis Higley had been employed by his father on the 78 acre farm; seven months later, when it was not fully cultivated, it was his responsibility. He promised to have all the land in cultivation within a fortnight. (Carpet Museum Trust)

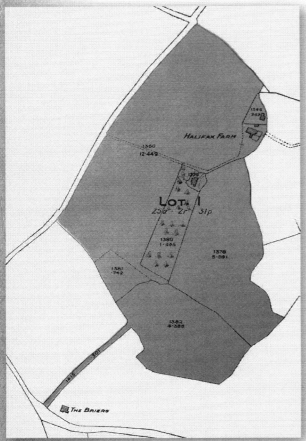

However, women remained the biggest pool of potential additional labour, and in spring 1916, 2,000 women volunteered for farm work in the county. Four months later the number had doubled. By July, local farms were well supplied with female labour. In 1917, the effects of the U-boat campaign and the indifferent harvest of the previous year raised the spectre of serious food shortages. Men and horses were both in short supply, and in September 1917 the County Food Production Committee urgently needed men for harvest work. Unfortunately they were constantly being re-examined for military purposes. Agriculture got the least fit men and, unless something was done at once, there would be hundreds of acres of unharvested corn in Worcestershire. This implied criticism of the women's efforts was not isolated. Mr Cox, a farmer running up to 400 sheep on his two farms, said that he employed women as far as possible 'but they didn't turn up when it was wet'. A farmer in the villages of Wolverley and Harvington claimed that 'women only wanted pianofortes and picture houses'.

In March 1917 there was an urgent appeal for motorists to drive motor tractors and man ploughs so that every available acre of arable land could be ploughed during the remaining weeks of the ploughing season (60). At the same time, the Worcestershire War Agricultural Executive Committee was allocated soldiers for agricultural work and 125 ploughmen and 180 other men with agricultural experience were assembled at Norton Barracks. A new campaign began the following month to recruit thousands more women to work on the land, and by August there were 1,022 full time and 1,891 part time female farmworkers in the county.

Wheat was increasingly reserved for making bread. By late 1916 it was illegal to use wheat to manufacture beer, the amount

SPEED THE PLOUGH.

An URGENT Appeal to Motorists for your Country's Vital Need—FOOD.

WE have been APPOINTED by the Commissioner of the Midlands under the Board of Agriculture, as ORGANIZERS in this District for the Distribution, Manning, Running, and Repairing of GOVERNMENT MOTOR PLOUGHS. The shortage of skilled labour immediately available can only be made good by VOLUNTEERS; THEREFORE

IT IS THE DUTY OF EVERY MOTORIST

to readily and IMMEDIATELY OFFER HIS OR HER SERVICES TO DRIVE A MOTOR TRACTOR AND MAN A PLOUGH.

Six weeks only are left

In which to do the work; in this time EVERY AVAILABLE ACRE OF ARABLE LAND SHOULD BE PLOUGHED.

What is required

(1) Two Motorists to Drive and Man each Machine (i.e.) one to Drive the Tractor and one to Guide the Plough (Day or Night).

(2) Volunteers with Cars to Drive the Workers to and from each Farm where Tractors are at Work (Day or Night),

[PETROL WILL BE AVAILABLE].

We are instructed to organize Three Shifts of Eight Hours each daily, for seven days a week. The proposed Shifts are as follows : 8 a.m. to 4 p.m. ; 4 p.m. to 12 midnight ; 12 midnight to 8 a.m. Or Four Shifts of Six Hours each might be more easily arranged to suit Volunteers. In either case the Ploughs must be kept at work ALL DAY and ALL NIGHT for the next six weeks.

The Government have fixed the Scale of Pay as follows : 4s. per shift of 8 hours plus 6d. per acre of Land Ploughed as certified by the Farmer. When Men do not work a full shift of 8 hours, wages will be calculated at 6d. per hour.

WE WANT **YOUR** HELP! MAY WE ENROL YOU?

Please reply by letter to L. C. GOODWIN, The Castle Motor Co., Ltd., Kidderminster

60. *An urgent appeal for motorists to help drive tractors and man ploughs in March 1917. The Castle Motor Company was co-ordinating this effort to maximise food production.* (Kidderminster Shuttle)

of flour that bakers could use for cakes and confectionery was restricted, and the use of cereals for animal feed was rationed. In May 1917 the Food Controller took over all the flour mills in the UK that used wheat, and the Food Economy Campaign suggested a voluntary ration of 3lb of flour per person per week. In addition, the flour was diluted with other grains, and eventually with soya and potato flour. Alternatives to wheat were promoted. In May 1917 Goodwin's advertised barley and maize flours, Harvey's advertised non-wheat flours, and a Royal Proclamation urged everyone 'to practice the greatest economy and frugality in the use of every species of grain'.

The supply of food did not just rely on the professional growers. Every available piece of land was used to grow food. As early as February 1915, Dalley's was telling the public how expensive vegetables were going to be and advising them to 'fill up every available space in your garden' with the help of instructions from '*Dalley's Garden Guide* (free on application)'. In 1916 the corporation set out a piece of land in Brinton Park near Sutton Road as allotments for an annual rent of 3*d* per perch. By June there were twenty-six allotment holders on the site. The acreage and number of allotment holders in Kidderminster increased by over 50 per cent (Fact box 23), a remarkable effort given the number of men who left the town and the additional work taken on by the remaining adults. Shorter shop and pub opening hours may have helped. This was part of a countrywide increase in allotments spurred by the food shortages of 1917.

The council encouraged poultry keeping by small holders, but stipulated no 'roosters'. Harvey's advertised fish meal called 'Mr Poultry-Feeder' stating that 'to be patriotic at this time, everyone should economise by purchasing the best foods at moderate price'. Once it was realised that an acre under potatoes would feed at least four times as many people as an acre under wheat, they

---

Fact box 23

ALLOTMENTS IN KIDDERMINSTER

Pre-war	96 acres (all private)	662 people
Added by Dec 1917	21 acres (mainly council)	188 people
Added by Apr 1918	28 acres (mainly council)	218 people
Total	145 acres	1,068 people

NO POTATOES.

T. WHEELER, 47 Offmore Road, not being able to get Vegetables for selling, will be glad to do light jobs with pony and truck, at reasonable charges, Post Cards will be promptly attended to.

became the focus of attempts to increase food production, especially on allotments. However, the main potato crop of 1916 was poor due to the lack of labour, horses and fertiliser. W.J. Wrigglesworth, of Mill Street, lent a quantity of seed potatoes to a farmer in Broome, but they were planted in barren moorland and there was no crop.

The resulting shortages were felt early the following year. One Saturday in March 1917 William E. Roberts, potato merchant and fruit and vegetable salesman in Coventry Street, sold 10 tons of potatoes with people queuing at his shop from 7.00 a.m. until after dark. The police had to regulate the crush of people. For those who did not want to queue, J.P. Harvey & Co. advertised white boiling peas as a cheap (2½d per lb) and nutritious substitute for scarce and dear potatoes. In May, Thomas Wheeler, greengrocer in Offmore Road, was unable to get any vegetables, especially potatoes, and had to find another way to earn a living (61).

When J.A. Bowdler, market gardener and fish dealer in the Horsefair, asked for an exemption from military service on the basis of his poor health, the clinching item was his promise to plant 3 acres of his land with potatoes. The potato crop of 1917 was unusually heavy, and in October the government bought the whole crop and resold it to dealers at fixed prices, usually 1d or 1¼d per pound. As with all foods, a substantial proportion was required for the armed forces and potatoes were dried and transported to the front to feed the soldiers.

Bread was a staple food, and demand increased to compensate for shortages of other foods. In 1915, the daily amount of bread per person at the workhouse was reduced by an ounce (to about 13oz) in response to the wartime shortages. Each inmate was consuming almost a loaf and a half a week. Bread prices increased several times, and by September 1917 a 4lb loaf

61. *By May 1917 the shortages were becoming serious.* (Kidderminster Shuttle)

cost 9*d*, with an extra halfpenny charged for delivery. The Co-op had five bread salesmen delivering, perhaps, 25,000 loaves a week to nearly 4,000 customers. By comparison, Alfred Leonard Smith, baker on Comberton Hill, produced 2,250 loaves, 200 Hovis loaves and other provisions each week.

At the Borough Court Frederick Walter Charles Smith, who ran a bakery and post office in Foley Park, was fined 40*s* for selling underweight bread. Any informer or customer, could check the weight of a loaf, prosecute and receive half of the fine, a useful source of extra income.

In January 1917 J.T. Pilling drew the attention of the tribunal to the high number of bread baking businesses in the town. Some men may have become bakers because it was a certified occupation or because it was a trade in which a good living could still be made in a wartime economy. Ninety-five men were registered as bakers under the Registration Act, but some of these had since joined the army or left the trade. The borough tribunal felt that 'there were more bakers in Kidderminster than were required in wartime.' Pilling submitted a scheme for pooling those bake houses in Kidderminster with suitable machinery to bake the bread for the town. These bakeries should run at their fullest capacity in order to keep their number as low as possible. It was calculated that no more than thirty-six bakers were required to meet the needs of the town's population. As there were fifty-five in the borough this would release nineteen for the army. Although the bakers grudgingly agreed to give the scheme a try, the tribunal eventually declined to accept any responsibility for it, claiming they fully appreciated the difficulties which existed, and urging the bakers to meet and come to some suitable arrangement.

Another essential was milk. The nineteen dairymen and milk sellers in Kidderminster before the war had only decreased by two in 1916. However, it is likely that their number fell further before the war ended as their requests for exemption from conscription began to be refused. Fear of a milk famine was expressed in the *Shuttle* as early as May 1916. As the reduction in farm labour affected what could be grown and the amount of fodder available, so milk shortages became a threat. The government's response was to control prices. In November 1916, price increases were limited to 6½d per gallon wholesale, and 2d per quart retail above pre-war prices. As there was still a strong seasonal element to milk supply with prices varying by the month this could not be further specified.

Efforts were made to make the milk go further. As early as August 1915 an advertisement from Meredith Brothers, grocers in the High Street, claimed the name was the only difference between their blue band margarine and pure butter, except for a saving of sixpence per pound. In October the government set the maximum retail price for milk in rural areas at 2s per gallon, rising to 2s 4d the following month until March 1918. In urban areas an extra 4d could be charged. As winter ended and the measures to increase farm output began to take effect, milk shortages eased locally, allowing prices to be reduced. By September 1918 it was 1s 3d per gallon.

By 1916 the number of butchers in the town had declined by 20 per cent, and many were struggling. Joseph Brown of Wood Street managed on his own, without even a boy to help him, having released two men for the army. Many shops selling meat imports were forced to close. The 'frozen ships' were used to transport food to the army rather than import meat. In 1917, German U-boat attacks on shipping caused substantial losses, and the population increasingly had to rely on home-grown meat, which was also needed to feed the troops. Hence, there were extensive campaigns to 'eat less meat'. Cheese, milk, peas, beans and lentils were all recommended as substitutes. A newspaper reported that meat 'in many homes is not much more than a Sunday luxury – except, perhaps, for the hard working father'. At Kidderminster's workhouse the daily meat consumption of each inmate was cut by an ounce to 4oz in 1915, saving over 2,500lb of meat in the course of the year.

The war forced changes in domestic pig farming. Cereal crops were reserved to feed the human population and brewing waste was curtailed, both of which had been used to feed pigs. The number of domestic pigs dropped, the price of bacon soared and pig breeding was encouraged.

By 1916 the tribunal considered that there were more slaughter men in the town than were needed and the Master Butchers Association was instructed to see what slaughter men could be spared for war service. Colonel Bertie reached an arrangement with the association and T.H. Roberts, slaughter man, and Arthur Baker, pork butcher in Blackwell Street, were given exemptions under the arrangement. However, A.R. Eaton, the Co-op's slaughter man, who should have enlisted under the arrangement, appealed on the grounds that single men had been exempted while he was a married man. He was given a conditional exemption. As a result, the arrangement was cancelled in June. Mr Field observed that, 'there had been too much jealousy between the Master Butchers' Association and the Co-operative Society'.

Sugar was extremely important for home baking and preserving. Before the war half the supplies were from Austria and Germany. As early as February 1915 it was suggested that refineries for sugar beet be established in England to avoid future importing from enemy countries. By September 1916 the shortage was serious. The Royal Commission on Sugar Supply retained about a quarter of the output of British refiners for the War Office. Refiners were instructed to issue the remainder only to their customers of 1915 and in the same proportions. Retailers were expected to distribute their supplies to their customers as fairly as possible. The sugar supply was expected to be no more than 75 per cent of the 1915 level. B.L. Griffiths, grocer in Swan Street, advertised 'good glucose', for use as a preserver while sugar was scarce, at a cost of 5½d per lb, or 5s 10d for a 14lb tin.

By 1917 food shortages were becoming acute. Prices were controlled, to prevent soaring inflation (Fact box 24). A 'Food Campaign' was launched in Kidderminster in April 1917 to reduce consumption of food, urging everyone to adopt a voluntary ration of 4lb of bread per person, per week. In May, adverts displayed the slogan 'save the bread and the bread will save you'. In some parts of the town, consumption of bread decreased by 25 per cent, but it was not enough, and rationing eventually had to be introduced.

A Food Control Committee was established in August 1917. It had powers to register local retailers of rationed items, oversee the number of customers registered with each retailer, and generally ensure that the rationing system worked well in their district. The first item to be rationed was sugar in December 1917, allowing ½lb of sugar per person, per week. In September, householders were informed that they needed to obtain a form, complete it, and send it to the local Food Control Committee. When returned, it was handed to their grocer who signed or stamped it with his name. Anyone failing to do this would be unable to get supplies of sugar. Although there was some confusion initially, the rationing was so successful at conserving stocks that in July 1918 extra sugar for jam-making was distributed.

> **Fact box 24**
>
> **ARTICLES UNDER THE FOOD CONTROLLER'S AUTHORITY, NOVEMBER 1917**
>
> Tea, sugar, butter, cheese, bacon, lard, farm oatmeal, rolled oats, green peas, split peas, split lentils, butter beans, currants, raisins, sultanas, oats, maize, maize semolina, corn flakes, barley, wheat, flour, self-raising flour, bread, meat, potatoes, milk, coal, matches, tobacco, cigarettes and cigars

In 1918 fats, butcher's meat and bacon were rationed. The ration books were 5in long and 4in wide, with separate cards of coupons for each food. They had a watermark and serial number to combat forgery. In all, 45 million ration books were printed, with another 18 million for the extra rations which were allowed to certain workers. They were introduced locally in May 1918. Meat could only be bought from the butcher with whom the purchaser had registered, and the ration card had to be produced. Each coupon allowed 5d worth of beef or mutton to be bought from the registered butcher, with no more than two coupons used per week. One coupon enabled the purchase of 5oz of bacon or ham, with up to four coupons used a week. Any 'unspent' coupons could be used to purchase tinned meat, rabbit, poultry or game.

At the end of September 1918 new ration books were issued covering the next twenty-six weeks. However, due to continuing shortages the value of the meat coupon was reduced to 4d. One coupon was needed for every 2oz of bacon and ham. Given that prices were still increasing, these changes represented substantial cuts in the meat allowance. When tea was rationed the allowance was at 1½oz.

There was also a serious shortage of coal and the men to handle it. In May 1916, H. Austin, coal merchant in Station Yard, had only two carters left, as five had enlisted. The eight boats and twenty-four men previously working the canal had reduced to five boats and eleven men. However, it was not just the numbers of men remaining that was a problem. Hauling required strong, fit and active men – exactly those required by the army. George Bradley, hauling munitions and coal, lost fifteen men to the armed forces and was left with old men and boys. When Arthur B. Pearson, a coal merchant in Station Yard, was fined at the Borough Court for delivering an underweight load, he claimed it was because his lack of men meant it had to be weighed on the railway station machine by a youth of 16, who was not always careful.

In June 1918 the shortages inspired the government to institute a system of 'National Kitchens' to supply simple but whole-some food, and maximise use of the sparse supplies of coal for cooking. Kidderminster's Food Economy Committee saw a great need for this type of help, as so many of the town's women were working and shortages of coal were making it difficult for families of all classes to provide hot meals. The unused Rifleman Inn, in the Horsefair (6), was considered a suitable venue and it was hoped to serve 500–1,000 meals a day. The kitchen was to be self-financing but not for profit and, eventually, supply two or three more centres in the borough with meals. About £500 was needed for equipment and alterations and an interest free loan from the government was to be repaid in ten annual instal-ments. The National Kitchen Department in London provided the kitchen utensils and other requirements. Mrs Anton was concerned to appoint an experienced and capable supervisor, and a good salary was offered. However, there was a shortage of labour for building alterations and installing electricity and there were delays in getting the equipment. The kitchens were not opened by Mrs Stanley Baldwin until 21 December, almost six weeks after the end of the war.

Inflation and the shortages caused real hardship for some. In February 1916 the workhouse had 391 male inmates, 173 women and twenty children. These were people who were too ill or infirm to work, and who were not entitled to the state pension which became available at age 70. High food prices meant hunger was a problem. Alfred Pitchford, aged 11, of Back Queen Street, was brought before the Children's Court for stealing a shilling from a little girl who had been sent on an errand by her mother. He admitted the theft and said he had spent the money on sweets and fish and chips. In May 1916, Henry Pearson, an old offender, stole a loaf of bread worth $4^{1}/_{2}d$ from the delivery boy of William T. Pearse, baker in Churchfields. Pearson admitted eating the loaf, and he was sent to gaol for twenty-one days.

Those with responsibilities towards the poor were acutely aware of the problems. In September 1916, at a meeting of the Board of Guardians, which had oversight of the workhouse and poor relief, the Rev. A. Gibson became animated. He 'did not hesitate to say that if anyone was found exploiting the trials and difficulties of the poor by unduly making money out of the food of the people they ought to be regarded as traitors to the country and should accordingly be shot'.

The government appreciated that there were problems and, in September 1916, a commissioner appointed for Worcestershire under the Military Service (Civil Liability) Committee, sat at the Town Hall to consider cases of special hardship. He dealt with a large number of applications from the residents of the district. The proceedings were so numerous that they lasted until dusk.

6

COMING HOME

At 11.00 a.m. on Monday, 11 November 1918 the Armistice sought by Germany came into effect (Fact box 25). Four and a quarter years of fighting was officially brought to a close. It came as a surprise to many (62). Brinton's Bull was sounded and the church bells were rung. Monday and Tuesday were declared public holidays and there were processions, fireworks and dancing in the streets. On Wednesday, a united service of thanksgiving was held in the Town Hall. Although only a cease-fire, it was popularly interpreted as a victory. The exhaustion of the warring countries and their economies meant resumption of hostilities was unlikely. The Town Council congratulated His Majesty and sang the National Anthem. In December a 'Great Victory Ball' was held at the Town Hall. The names of the fallen were read at a Day of Remembrance for all denominations at St Mary's Church.

Conscription and the tribunal were immediately suspended. Although munitions work was no longer necessary, other conditions of exemption, such as maintaining soldiers' businesses or as Special Constables, were continued.

Between 702,000 and 740,000 British servicemen died during the war. Some died frustratingly close to the Armistice.

Fact box 25

TERMS OF THE ARMISTICE, 1918

Germany to:

- Evacuate all occupied territory.
- Evacuate all soldiers from the west bank of the Rhine.
- Surrender military equipment.
- Place their submarines and fleet in allied hands.
- Repudiate the treaties ending the war on the eastern front.
- Pay reparations for war damage.
- Accept the continuing Allied blockade of German ports.

By direction of the CASTLE MOTOR Co., Ltd., who require the whole of their Premises for the Manufacture of Munitions.

On TUESDAY, NOVEMBER 12th,
At Twelve o'clock sharp,
AT THE SHOW ROOMS, VICAR STREET,
KIDDERMINSTER,

LEONARD A. OUSTON

IS instructed by the Castle Motor Co., Ltd., who require the whole of their premises for the Manufacture of Munitions, to SELL BY AUCTION (without reserve), the Stock of

MOTOR CARS

62. Advert of 9 November 1918. By the time of the sale, peace had arrived and the expansion of munitions was no longer needed. (Kidderminster Shuttle)

Captain Charles H. Crowe, born in Claughton Street but living in Philadelphia, died of wounds three hours before the Armistice.

Many families still did not know what had happened to their loved ones. In August 1919, the parents of missing Private Walter Thomas Powell, 2nd Battalion Essex Regiment, were told he must now be presumed killed on 20 April 1918. Before the war he had worked at Baldwin's Stour Vale Works. Rifleman F.A. Bennett of Lorne Street, in 1/17th London Regiment, reported missing since 23 March 1918 was, over a year later, presumed to have died on that day. The dependents of all deceased soldiers were paid small allowances by the army. Under the Regimental Debts Act of 1893, the army pay owed to deceased servicemen of the Worcestershire Regiments was to be paid to their relatives, and applications were invited in April 1919.

There was another killer: October 1918 saw the start of a deadly epidemic of influenza which attacked previously healthy young adults. Its development and spread were closely linked to the crowded, mobile and unhealthy conditions in which the soldiers lived. It quickly infected the civilian population, and killed about 200,000 people in England and Wales. In Kidderminster, all schools were closed between 22 October and 18 November and cinemas were disinfected. The Poor Law Institution banned visitors. The Medical War Commission was asked to release doctors from the army, as those in the town were overwhelmed with the work. Between 19 October and 7 December 1918, the period when the disease was at its height, there were 128 deaths from influenza in Kidderminster, and many more were infected. There was a double funeral for flu victims Thomas Hunter and his wife who ran the Cape of Good Hope Inn, New Road. Their daughter, Dolly, also suffered.

Demobilisation took a long time (63). Tradesmen vital for the rebuilding of the peacetime economy were released first. Lieutenant Ernest Phipps of the Royal Army Service Corps, was back with his firm Clibbery & Phipps, auctioneers and valuers at Bank Buildings, in December 1918 (64). An emergency employment exchange was established in the Arch Hill Baptist Sunday School. When companies needed labour the Demobilisation Sub-committee, chaired by Alderman G.W. Grosvenor, put pressure on the government to release suitable servicemen.

63. Demobilisation papers of Francis Cyril Thompson. (Melvyn Thompson)

NOTICE.   NOTICE.   NOTICE.

ALBERT CHERRILL,

HAIRDRESSER and TOBACCONIST,

Begs to announce that he has been discharged from H M Forces, and IS NOW CARRYING ON BUSINESS AS USUAL at the same address

24, PARK BUTTS,

and wishes to thank the public for past patronage, and hopes to merit their confidence in the future.

KIDDERMINSTER

WATCH REPAIRING DEPOT,

1, PARK BUTTS.

G. KING has the pleasure to announce that he has RETURNED TO BUSINESS at the above address. He specialises in high-class Watch, Clock, and Jewellery REPAIRS, including Gilding and Engraving.

All Work done on the Premises.

64. *The men who survived resumed their old occupations. These adverts appeared in January 1919.* (Kidderminster Shuttle)

Soldiers were also needed to dismantle the military machine. The 1/7th Worcesters, who had been in northern Italy fighting the Austrians, were sent to Taranto, in the south, to guard British stores. Their commander, Lieutenant Colonel F.M. Tomkinson, DSO, thanked local contributors to the Christmas Dinner Fund. Their journey home started in late March 1919 and they arrived at Kidderminster on the afternoon of 2 April. The mayor greeted them at the station and, amid great enthusiasm, they marched to their headquarters at the Shrubbery. At 5.00 p.m. the colours were marched off and the parade was

Fact box 26

VC CITATION FOR JOHN FRANCIS YOUNG, PRIVATE, 87TH QUEBEC REGIMENT

'For most conspicuous bravery and devotion to duty in attack at Dury-Arras sector on 2nd September 1918, when acting as a stretcher-bearer attached to 'D' Company.

The Company in the advance over the ridge suffered heavy casualties from shell and machine-gun fire. Private Young, in spite of the complete absence of cover, without the least hesitation went out, and in the open fire-swept ground dressed the wounded. Having exhausted his stock of dressings, on more than one occasion he returned, under intense fire, to the Company headquarters for a further supply. This work he continued for over an hour, displaying throughout the most absolute fearlessness.

To his courageous conduct must be ascribed the saving of the lives of many of his comrades. Later, when the fire had somewhat slackened, he organised and led stretcher parties to bring in the wounded whom he had dressed. All through the operations of 2nd, 3rd, and 4th September Private Young continued to show the greatest valour and devotion to duty.'

His medal is in the Canadian War Museum.

dismissed. The soldiers were finally able to disperse to their homes.

However, over 1,500 Kidderminster men were still waiting to be demobilised. The local Parents' League held an open air meeting in September 1919 to, 'call upon the government to release all conscripts under 21 years of age'. Nationally, the process was not completed until 1922.

Some men chose to continue serving. In January 1920, Captain Wilfred Tomkinson CB, MVO, staff officer to the commander of the battlecruiser squadron, was appointed captain of the newly commissioned HMS *Hood*, the latest and longest fighting ship and largest warship in the world. He was Michael Tomkinson's third son.

For most families the return of the soldiers was a joyful occasion. In September 1919, Mr and Mrs G. Barlow celebrated the return of their youngest son, Fred, from France. Their third son was home on leave from Germany, and their eldest daughter was visiting from Worcester, Massachusetts.

Especially honoured were the men who had been awarded Victoria Crosses. Private John Francis Young, a native of Kidderminster and old boy of St George's School, received his Victoria Cross from the King, at Buckingham Palace on 30 April 1919 (Fact box 26). He had emigrated to Canada, where he worked for the Imperial Tobacco Company, and joined 87th Battalion Quebec Regiment. Young was honoured at a meeting of the War Memorial Committee in the Town Hall and a presentation was made to him at St George's School.

Served with honour and was disabled in the Great War.

Honourably discharged on 22nd November 19.

No. 9691. Pte. Arthur Osborne Blent.
Worcestershire Regiment.

George R.I.

Many soldiers came home disabled (65). G. Moule of Yew Tree Road, a steam finisher and packer in the carpet industry, suffered from chronic rheumatism. The pension paid to disabled soldiers depended on their degree of disability. In September 1918, the Comrades of the Great War opened a club house with reading and billiards rooms in Swan Street. It already had 150 members. Over twenty local soldiers died of their war injuries between 1919 and 1921 (see Profile 4).

As the fighting ceased, the need for facilities for the injured reduced. The Larches Red Cross Hospital held a farewell concert, whist drive and dance in April 1919, before closing at the end of the month. The town took pride in the treatment of wounded soldiers at the infirmary and a certificate of thanks from the Army Council, signed by Winston Churchill, was well received.

65. *The king sent certificates of appreciation to all those who returned wounded. (Roger Matthews)*

A.O. BLENT, PRISONER OF WAR

Arthur Osborne Blent, born in Hoobrook, was orphaned early in life and admitted to Old Swinford Hospital in 1889, aged 10. He was apprenticed in Kidderminster in 1893, aged 14, first to an ironmonger and then to a house painter. He served in the Boer War and married May immediately afterwards.

When war broke out again he enlisted on 3 November 1914 and joined 3rd Worcesters. He was paid 1s 3d per day.

He wrote two letters to his daughter, Lilly, from Raglan Barracks where he was training:

> I don't think I shall be able to come home at Christmas … Glad you have got a raincoat so you will be able to go to Chapel and Sunday school when it is wet. … Hope you will have lots of pudding and cake at Christmas. Hope Norman is better and Harry is a better boy. … Thank you for the stamps.

> Glad to hear that Gladys has got better from the measles … Hope the peppermints you sent to the soldiers they will enjoy. Thank mamma for cigarettes. … I think you get quite good at writing letters, and with a little more practice you will be all right … From your Ever loving dad.

He was drafted to France in 1915, and sent Lilly the souvenir postcard pictured. During fighting in the Somme area he was partially gassed. He was 'missing' for a long time, before his family learnt that he had been taken prisoner. After the war the prisoners returned to Kidderminster by train. The family members who went to meet them were warned in advance not to show too much expression at their poor physical state. Arthur was assessed at 20 per cent disablement and paid a weekly pension of 13s 10d for himself, his wife and three children.

CARTE POSTALE

POST CARD ✳ POSTKAART

CORRESPONDANCE

Dear Lilly I am sending
you a card I hope you will
like it. I expect you
are looking forward to
leaving school for good
I am quite well hoping
you are from your dad xx

ADRESSE

Miss L Blent
19 Broad St
Kidderminster
Worcestershire
England

(Roger Mathews)

Many soldiers had been prisoners in Germany and Turkey (Profile 7). In November, Mrs Whaile of Northumberland Avenue heard that her son, A.J. Whaile, taken prisoner at Katia, had arrived at Alexandria and would soon be home. Private W. Reynolds of Rackfield Avenue, was a prisoner of the Germans for three years. He and his colleagues had walked 40 miles to France to receive care from the Red Cross. He was leaving for England on 25 November. Lieutenant R.J. Pritchard of Chester Road, was the first officer to return home after being one of 600 prisoners of war held at Mainz in Germany. He had been captured on 21 March 1918, on the first day of the German offensives. Disappointingly, it was learned that the prisoners had not received the large quantities of food and money sent to them through the local prisoner-of-war fund. Remaining monies in local funds for soldiers were transferred to the Old Comrades Association of the Worcestershire Regiment, for ex-prisoners' benefit.

Many of the men who came home from the war had lost their livelihoods, or were not capable of resuming their pre-war work. In February 1919, with £80,000, the king started a fund to help discharged servicemen become self-supporting. At least £3,000,000 was required. The mayor appealed locally for donations, and a national scheme to employ disabled ex-servicemen was supported by thirty-six local employers. Injured men were to form 2 per cent of the workforce at Tomkinson & Adam, who had started employing injured soldiers during the war. However, as ex-employees returned to their old jobs, the scheme had to be abandoned by Brinton's. Partially disabled men could not be dismissed by their employers without reference to the Kidderminster War Pensions Committee.

Food Control and Rationing continued well after the war. In December 1918 restrictions were removed from some meats and sausages, while coupons for other meats were doubled in value. The price of eggs was still fixed, jam was still rationed and tea still had to be obtained from the registered supplier. Sugar rations were increased to ¾lb, and organisers of entertainments for children or wounded servicemen were allowed an ounce of sugar per person. By January 1919, supplies to manufacturers were returned to their 1915 levels. In November 1918, a meeting chaired by the mayor proposed to approach the government to build a sugar beet factory in Kidderminster. Local farmers had already agreed to supply the sugar beet as local soil was ideal. It was opened in December 1925.

Although margarine was taken out of food control on 8 March 1919, there was an acute shortage of butter and, in August 1919, the ration was reduced to 1½oz per person, per week. Registration of customers with retailers for ham, bacon and lard ceased, but price controls remained in place. Food Control Committees continued until at least 30 June 1920, and 26,000 new ration books/cards were issued in autumn 1919. People were still being prosecuted for breaching the rules: W.A. Howarth, milk merchant of Blackwell Street, was fined for selling milk above the maximum price in March 1919, and in October 1919 George Birkin Clarke, butcher in High Street, was fined £40 for profiteering in meat, selling it at 1s 10d per lb instead of 1s 6d per lb.

66. The tank and two guns given to Kidderminster were displayed in Brinton's Park. (Carpet Museum Trust)

However, the local economy was expanding. Certificates were granted to a number of people to sell bacon, including Kate Whale of Stourbridge Road, grocer, and George Hart of George Street, shopkeeper. Alice Bicknell in Stourbridge Road and Annie Young in the Horsefair, shopkeepers, were granted certificates to sell milk. Supplies of fuel were increasing and the Electric Company promised that supplies would be more plentiful – during the war there had been long stoppages on the tramway system, and loss of lighting in the town with many carpet companies losing working time due to loss of power. Petrol supplies improved, and cars were brought back into use.

However, fuel supplies were not yet meeting the demand, and inflation continued. Children had to wear their coats in school due to the shortage of heating. In July 1919, the cost of coal was increased by 6s per ton, and in October, a Gas and Coal Emergency Order required Kidderminster Gas Company to reduce off peak gas pressure, and consumers were requested to use gas with all possible economy.

By 1922 there were signs of depression. The price of gas was reduced and the local Chamber of Commerce requested a reduction in the cost of postage to aid recovery. The government still needed money, and the sale of war bonds continued. A 'Thanksgiving Gun Week' was held in January 1919 – a 6in Howitzer, weighing 4 tons, was presented in recognition of the town's achievement and a captured German gun was promised. In August, the National War Savings Committee presented the town with a 28 ton tank, directly from the battlefields. After a handing-over ceremony at the Rowland Hill Statue, it was driven round the streets and put on a prepared plinth in Brinton's Park (66). (It was broken up for scrap

Fact box 27

THE TERMS OF THE TREATY OF VERSAILLES
Germany was to:

- Accept responsibility for provoking the war.
- Surrender Alsace-Lorraine to France.
- Enable the re-establishment of Poland.
- Give Belgium towns in the Ardennes.
- Allow the Saar Valley to be placed under international control.
- Demilitarise the Rhineland and Heligoland.
- Mandate overseas colonies to the Allied countries.
- Severely reduce its military capability.
- Pay reparations of £6,500 million.

The League of Nations was established.

in 1940 for the Second World War.) By February 1921 a total of £1,560,999 had been invested in the town, more than £60 per head of population.

Peace was concluded with the signing of the Treaty of Versailles on 28 June 1919 (Fact box 27). The German fleet was surrendered, the payment of reparations imposed, the League of Nations established and German colonies became League Mandates, many under British control. There were plans to celebrate the anticipated signing. In June 1919, the Peace Celebrations Committee decided to give a dinner to all sailors, soldiers and airmen of Kidderminster and asked the men to register with J.H. Thursfield, who had resumed his post as Town Clerk. The Free Church League warned its members against participation, because 'the peace terms fail most lamentably to show the spirit which Christians are enjoined to show to their enemies, and we know that peace on such terms can be no peace'. Empire Thanksgiving Day was declared for 6 July, and 19 July was to be a day of public rejoicing.

The peace celebrations included the dinner for discharged servicemen at 12.30 in Brinton's Park, sports for them in the afternoon, a procession of children from the Town Hall to Brinton's Park, followed by sports for them, with bands performing during the day and dancing at night, rounded off by a bonfire at 10.00 p.m. (Fact box 28). However, rain disrupted some of the events, and the behaviour of some of the men got out of hand when beer and the meat from the ox roasting were distributed, and again when the cigarettes and matches made their appearance.

In August 1919 Alderman Tomkinson entertained over 1,000 workpeople of Tomkinson & Adam at their own peace celebration at Franche Hall.

Fact box 28

PEACE CELEBRATIONS

Receipts

Transfer from Prisoner-of-war fund	£874 9s 4d
Sundry sales	£277 7s 7d
Special grant from Borough Fund	£500 0s 0d
Total	**£1,651 16s 11d**

Payments

Dinner to ex-soldiers	£625 15s 1d
Teas to school children	£392 12s 1d
Decorations	£66 10s 0d
Amusements	£118 8s 9d
Ox roasting	£13 1s 2d
Surveyor's Dept. (wages)	£61 14s 2d
Miscellaneous	£156 7s 5d
Total	**£1,434 8s 8d**

Balance	**£217 8s 3d**

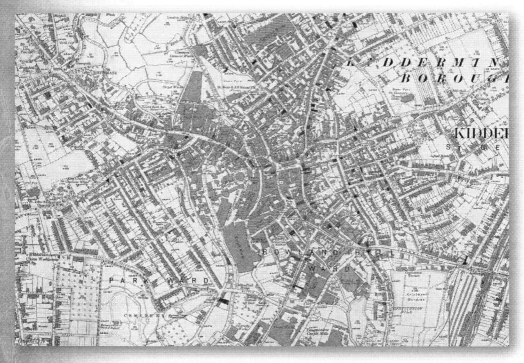

An enlargement of the 1902 map of Kidderminster. (Worcestershire Archives and Archaeology)

Postscript

Legacy

During the war, Herbert Smith, owner of Carpet Trades (see Fact box 2), chaired the Carpet Materials and Rationing Committee for the town, as well as manufacturing substantial amounts of material for the war effort. In the Birthday Honours of 1920 he was created a baronet. He took his employees to Tewkesbury to celebrate, and presented the Military Medal to Gunner H. Pheasey. He used his profits from the war effort to buy Witley Court, where he lived until it burnt down on the eve of the Second World War.

With peace came the need to return to peacetime production. The government started selling its surplus stores and buildings in July 1919. Kidderminster's factories returned to making carpets. George Rainsford, company secretary of Greatwich Limited, had joined the Artists' Rifles Regiment. As Captain Rainsford, OBE and bar, he was welcomed back at a director's meeting on 6 March 1919. He joined H.L.J. Greatwich (the founder's son) and Harry Westcott in running the company, but the bank took control and Greatwich left. In spite of their problems, the company gave a bonus to their employees, including the returned soldiers, and £50 was given to Kidderminster War Memorial fund. A few years later, Rainsford and Westcott were able to buy the company back from the bank. When Westcott retired the company continued in the hands of Rainsford and his son.

Three years after the end of hostilities the local carpet industry entered a short period of growth and prosperity. Although a big demand for raw materials meant costs soared, it rapidly recovered and the export trade was strong. Factories expanded, with new facilities underway at Tomkinson & Adam, Naylor's, Greatwich and Carpet Manufacturing Co. in 1921. Every available loom in the town was operating, with strong home and export markets. Wages were 150 per cent higher than in 1913 and, although productivity was only 30 per cent of 1913 levels, income was high. However, production dropped by over a third in 1922, as economic depression set in. Baldwin's continued to expand, in both Britain and Canada, and by 1921 they had forty properties and nine subsidiary companies. However, while dividends paid on shares since the start of the war had been consistent, they shrank in 1921 and were not paid at all in 1922.

After the war, with the return of the soldiers and the closure of the munitions factories, jobs were again at a premium. Wages were expected to fall with the end of the war bonuses, although their three months peacetime payment did not start until the peace treaty was signed. When, in April 1919, the workhouse advertised for a probationer nurse the salary was £10 with board and lodging plus a war bonus of £10 during the continuance of the war. Those in work wanted to protect their jobs. The county magistrates rejected the idea of employing women in the police force, and the unions rejected proposals to train disabled sailors and soldiers as engineers or weavers.

In April 1919, Mrs J.H. Prunell of Holman Street, who had worked for nearly two and a half years in the Town Clerk's office, left because her husband had been demobilised. Women's resumption of their pre-war roles did not mean that there were jobs for the returning soldiers. In July, the Kidderminster Labour Exchange reported that there were very few women workers on the fund but about 600 discharged soldiers were receiving assistance.

In 1920, a number of Kidderminster people emigrated to Toronto, Canada, to help develop their carpet industry.

Unemployment continued in spite of the prosperity in the home carpet industry, and in January 1921 there were 854 men and 62 women on the register. The National Unemployment Grants Committee promised funds to help – but preference had to be given to unemployed ex-servicemen. By July 1921 there were 1,468 unemployed men. The mayor started a fund for the relief of distress amongst the unemployed. Nationally, unemployment approached 11 per cent, and there was a decade of deflation and stagnation.

Not all the soldiers had a happy welcome from their families (Profile 8). Walter Bertram Onslow, a fishmonger and greengrocer in Wood Street and Mill Street, had been conscripted in 1917 leaving his wife in Kidderminster. After being demobbed in 1919 he found she had gone to Birmingham with another man. At a divorce hearing the co-respondent said he believed the husband had 'been knocked out in the war'. Lawrence Cyril Smith, baker on Comberton Hill, was prepared to give his brother, who had served in Mesopotamia and India, rooms above the bakery. However, family arguments over money, rent and accommodation ended up in court.

The Representation of the People Act 1918 (Fact box 29) effectively trebled the electorate. This was a result of the democratising effect of the war – the bullet did not discriminate, and people at all levels of society did their bit for the war effort. The Labour Party was a major beneficiary. Locally, in the council elections of November 1919, they put up five candidates. Two were elected: Louis Tolley defeated Reginald S. Brinton in Rowland Hill Ward, and Harold Gould defeated Ellis W. Talbot in Park Ward. Did the new electorate dislike the defeated men's role in the tribunal? Councillor Tolley's employer refused to allow him time off for council meetings and gave him a week's notice, and a week later he had been employed by Brinton, his defeated opponent.

Legislation also enabled women to stand for election. In June 1919, the Women's Citizens Association announced that Helen Talbot would stand for St George's Ward in the forthcoming Town Council by-election. By September 1919 there was a women's section of the Kidderminster

> **Fact box 29**
>
> **REPRESENTATION OF THE PEOPLE ACT, 1918**
>
> All men over 21 given the vote (almost doubling the male electorate).
>
> Women over 30 given the vote provided they were:
>
> - Ratepayers or wives of ratepayers,
> - Property owners,
> - Or graduates voting in a University constituency.

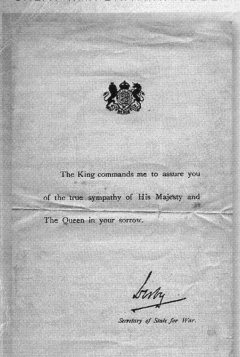

The King commands me to assure you

of the true sympathy of His Majesty and

The Queen in your sorrow.

Derby

Secretary of State for War.

Labour Party. Women's participation in public life was taken a step further when the Sex Disqualification Removal Act enabled women to be JPs (see Profile 2).

The war prompted many memorials. In 1919 a memorial café was opened on Station Hill by J. Harvey in memory of his son, John Percival Harvey of the Worcestershire Yeomanry, who died in Damascus. The dead were commemorated with medals known as 'Widows' Pennies' (67). Locally, medals and certificates were issued to about 400 mothers and widows of men killed in the war (49). The Old Carolians placed a memorial grandfather clock in the school hall, and a war memorial in the St John's Institute was unveiled by Rev. D.H.S. Mould.

67. The Widows' Penny and King's Note of Sympathy commemorating Jack Watkins. They were sent to the relatives of those who died. (Bob and Phill Millward)

68. *The figure of Peace, sculpted by Alfred Drury, RA, as the focal point of Kidderminster's war memorial. (Photo: Sally Dickson)*

WILLIAM THOMAS BAYES, A NEW LIFE AT HOME

William Thomas Bayes was born in Blackwell Street in 1886. He spent his working life at Tomkinson's Carpet factory in the dye shop.

In 1909 he married Esther Jane Reynolds and a daughter, Ethel May Bayes, was born in 1911. Two more children died in infancy: Ivy M. Reynolds Bayes, born in December 1912, died six months later, and then Charles T. Reynolds Bayes, born in June 1914, died the same month.

William volunteered early in the war. He is seen here in uniform, in a studio setting that imitates a painting. He served with distinction in the Royal Horse Artillery. He suffered frostbite in the trenches, and after recuperation he returned to the front and served until the Armistice. By then, he was a driver in the Royal Field Artillery.

In 1916 he came home on leave, and discovered that his wife, Esther, had been unfaithful. After demobilisation, William, who lived in Lark Hill, sought a divorce which was granted early in 1922. At that time divorces were sufficiently unusual to be reported in the local paper.

In December 1917 Esther gave birth to a son, Charles A. Reynolds Lawrence. After the divorce she married Joseph Arthur Lawrence, and another son was born in Birmingham in 1926, Harold N. Reynolds Lawrence.

In 1925 William married Elizabeth Kimberlin in Kidderminster – a much happier marriage with surviving family. An essentially modest man, William refused to talk about his First World War experiences, apart from admitting that he and his colleagues were distressed at the deaths of so many horses. He did, however, confess that the whole experience was 'horrible'.

He served his country again in the Second World War by fire-watching and munitions work in Tomkinson's bomb shop.

His medals are in the care of the Imperial War Museum.

(Mrs James)

69. *The yard of George Brown & Sons, where the panels of names for Kidderminster's war memorial were carved, showing the figure for Lye war memorial almost finished. (Catherine and Peggy Guest)*

In June 1919, Kidderminster's War Memorial Committee adopted three options: a public memorial including the names of the fallen, expansion of Kidderminster Infirmary and Children's Hospital, and Comrades of the Great War Club. The estimated cost was £41,500. However, the economy was contracting, and by October 1919 only £1,123 16s had been donated. The three-part scheme was abandoned in favour of the public memorial. Peter Adam approached Alfred Drury RA, sculptor, who chose a site in the centre of the road near St Mary's Church. He proposed a bronze, winged figure of Peace on a Portland stone base, with an inscription on the front and brass plates on three sides containing up to 450 names of the local fallen.

By 1921, the estimated cost had doubled to £3,000 and there was great difficulty raising the money. A list of all those who had donated was published in mid-January, headed by the manufacturers, who donated up to £275 each, followed by employees, schools, councillors and many private individuals. By the end of the month £2,427 3s 10d had been raised.

In February 1922, the committee decided to use the following words on the memorial:

These died the noblest death a man may die
Fighting for God and Right and Liberty,
And such a death is immortality
[From a poem by John Oxenham]

So they passed over and all the trumpets
Sounded for them on the other side
[Based on John Bunyan's description of the death of pilgrim, Valiant-for-Truth]

They were to be placed adjacent to the list of the names of the fallen. It was decided not to include the military ranks of the fallen soldiers.

By February 1922 Alfred Drury was working on the statue, and the child was finished (68). However, donations did not yet cover the cost. In August a 'Shilling Appeal' was launched for the last £250 required. J.H. Thursfield, committee secretary, and George Eddy each gave 200s. A delay was caused by problems over the design, the increased price of raw materials and the doubling of the number of panels to accommodate 800 names. These were eventually placed on a separate stand, sculpted by George Brown & Sons (69). On 22 October, the Earl of Coventry performed the official unveiling of the memorial. The Bishop of Worcester was in attendance, together with the

Fact box 30

WAR MEMORIALS IN KIDDERMINSTER

Kidderminster town memorial	661 names
St Mary's Church	320 names
Baxter United Reform Church	34 names
Hoobrook	39 names
St John's Church	147 names
Milton Hall Baptists	10 names
New Meeting	13 names
St Ambrose Church	34 names
Conservative & Unionist Club	18 names
St George's Church	12 names
Total number of names recorded	742

NB: Some names were recorded on up to four memorials. 249 of these deaths were not reported in the *Kidderminster Shuttle*.

70. *The dedication of Kidderminster's war memorial on 22 October 1922. (Carpet Museum Trust)*

71. The war memorial inside St Mary's Church, with the metal grille open showing the volume containing the Roll of Honour. (Photo: Sally Dickson)

civic dignitaries. The military was represented, and all those who had lost a family member in the war came and laid tributes on the memorial (70).

Several local churches funded war memorials for the fallen soldiers from their congregations (Fact box 30), including the parish church of St Mary's. Originally intended to take the form of a chancel screen recording the names of the fallen, designer Gilbert Scott chose a monument for the north wall. A central figure of Victory holds an uplifted sword and laurel wreath.

72. *The Colours of 7th Battalion Worcestershire Regiment Territorial Army, showing their Battle Honours from two world wars. They were laid up on 28 January 1967 when the battalion was disbanded. (Photo: Sally Dickson)*

Above are St George and Joan of Arc, representing the heroism of the men and women in the war. Below, a niche fitted with a gilded metal grille holds a volume containing an illuminated Roll of Honour. The monument is of grey Forest of Dean stone, alabaster and 'rosso antico' marble (71). Adjacent are the colours of the 7th Worcesters, recording their battle honours from two world wars (72).

In October 1919, Lord Cecil asked every city, town and village to celebrate 11 November, the anniversary of Armistice Day, as League of Nations Day. Commemorations on this date have continued ever since. It is now known as Remembrance Day.

BIBLIOGRAPHY

Barber, R., *Images of England: Kidderminster*, Tempus, 1999.
Barber, R., *Images of England: Kidderminster – The Second Selection*, Tempus, 2002.
Barry, G., & Carruthers, A., *A History of Britain's Hospitals*, Book Guild, 2005.
Bennett's Business Directory: Worcestershire, 1914.
Bishop, A., & Bostridge, M., *Letters From a Lost Generation*, Little, Brown & Co., 1998.
Butler, R., & Gilbert, D., *For Valour: Kidderminster's Four V.C.s*, Kidderminster, 2000.
Cambell-Smith, D., *Masters of the Post: The Authorized History of the Royal Mail*, Penguin, 2011.
Chinn, C., 'Invention that Changed Leisure Habits of a Nation', in *Express and Star*, 28.3.2013.
Colquhoun, K., *Taste: The Story of Britain through its Cooking*, Bloomsbury, 2007.
Doyle, P., *The British Soldier of the First World War*, Shire, 2008.
Doyle, P., *British Postcards of the First World War*, Shire, 2010.
Doyle, P., *First World War Britain*, Shire, 2012.
Galloway, P., *The Order of the British Empire*, 1996.
Gilbert, B.B., *David Lloyd George, A Political Life: The Organizer of Victory 1912–16*, Batsford, 1992.
Gilbert, D., *The Kidderminster War Memorial 1922–2007*, Kidderminster War Memorials Conservation Trust, 2007.
Gilbert, N., *Ridiculous Refinement: The Mansions of the Kidderminster Carpet Barons*, Hencroft Press, 2001.
Gilbert, N., *A History of Kidderminster*, Phillimore, 2004.
Hogg, I.V., *The Guns 1914–18*, Pan Books, 1971.
Ireland, B., *War at Sea 1914–45*, Cassell, 2002.
James, L., *Warrior Race: A History of the British at War*, Little, Brown & Co., 2001.
Keegan, J., *Opening Moves August 1914*, Pan Books, 1971.
Keegan, J., *The First World War*, Hutchinson, 1998.

Kelly's Directories, 1912, 1916, 1924.

London Gazette.

Manuals of Emergency Legislation: Food (Supply and Production) Manuals, HMSO, 1913–1918.

Marchant, J., Bryan, R., & Alcock, J., *Bread: a Slice of History*, The History Press, 2008.

Marsh, A., *The Carpet Weavers of Kidderminster: A History of the Power Loom Carpet Weavers and Textile Workers Union of Kidderminster*, Malthouse Publishing, 1995.

McNab, C., *Tommy: First World War Soldier*, Pitkin, 2012.

Messenger, C., *Trench Fighting 1914–18*, Pan Books, 1972.

Nowell-Smith, S., *Edwardian England 1901–1914*, Oxford U.P., 1964.

Opie, R., *The 1910s Scrapbook: The Decade of the Great War*, New Cavendish Books, 2000.

Parliamentary Debates, Hansard: House of Commons Official Report.

Phillips, M., *The Ascent of Woman: A History of the Suffragette Movement and the Ideas Behind It*, Little, Brown, 2003.

Pope, R., *The British Economy Since 1914: A Study in Decline?*, Longman, 1998.

Porter, R., *The Greatest Benefit to Mankind: A Medical History of Humanity from Antiquity to the Present*, Harper Collins, 1997.

Public and General Acts, HMSO, 1914–18

Pugh, R.M., *Kidderminster Shuttle Index of Great War Casualties 1914–1921*, compiled 2001.

Robertson, J., *New Zealand in the First World War 1914–18*, Reed Publishing, 1938.

Salaman, R.N., *The History and Social Influence of the Potato*, Cambridge U.P., 1949 revised 1985.

Smith, P., New Meeting Church Kidderminster: First World War Memorial, (undated).

Stacke, H. FitzM., *The Worcestershire Regiment in the Great War*, Cheshires,1929.

Statutory Rules and Orders, HMSO, 1914–1918.

Storey, N.R., & Housego, M., *Women in the First World War*, Shire, 2010.

The British Medical Journal.

The First World War Experienced, Open University, 2014.

The Illustrated War Record, Headley, undated (c.1917).

The Oxford History of the British Army, Oxford U.P., 1994.

The Times.

The Times Atlas of European History, Times Books, 1994.

The Village Atlas: The Growth of Birmingham and the West Midlands 1831–1907, The Village Press, 1989.

The Worcestershire Regiment – A Brief History, Worcestershire Regimental Museum, (undated, after 1970).

Thompson, M., *Woven in Kidderminster*, David Voice Associates, 2002.

Thompson, M., *Mills and Tall Chimneys of Kidderminster*, Hencroft Press, 2012.

Thompson, M., & Voice, D., *The Illustrated History of Kidderminster and Stourport Electric Tramway Company 1898–1929*, David Voice Associates, 1998.

Tomkinson, K., *Characters of Kidderminster*, Kenneth Tomkinson Ltd, 1977.

Tomkinson, K., & Hall, G., *Kidderminster Since 1800*, Kenneth Tomkinson Ltd, 1985.

War 1914: Punishing the Serbs, The Stationery Office, 1999.

Way, T., *Allotments*, Shire, 2008.

Winstanley, M.J., *The Shopkeeper's World 1830–1914*, Manchester University Press, 1983.

Woods, A., 'Rethinking the History of Modern Agriculture: British Pig Production c.1910–65', in *Twentieth Century British History*, vol.23, no.2, Oxford U.P., 2012.

Additional sources accessed online:

Ancestry.com

Australian Light Horse Studies Centre

Baker, C., The Long, Long Trail

Cricket Archive

Familysearch.org

Free BMD

Genesreunited

Geni.com

Google maps

Household Books

Imperial War Museum

Kidderminster Civic Society: Historic Kidderminster Project, Building Reports

Kingsley, N., Landed Families of Britain and Ireland

National Army Museum

Spink Auctions

Victoria and Albert Museum

Victoriacross.org

A Vision of Britain Through Time

Wikipedia.org

Worcestercitymuseums.org

Worcestershireregiment.com

Great War Britain:
The First World War at Home

Luci Gosling

After the declaration of war in 1914, the conflict
dominated civilian life for the next four years. Magazines
quickly adapted without losing their gossipy essence:
fashion jostled for position with items on patriotic
fundraising, and court presentations were replaced by
notes on nursing. The result is a fascinating, amusing and
uniquely feminine perspective of life on the home front.

978 0 7524 9188 2

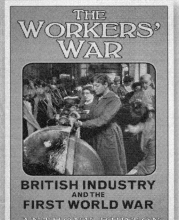

The Workers' War:
British Industry and the First World War

Anthony Burton

The First World War didn't just rock the nation in terms
of bloodshed: it was a war of technological and industrial
advances. Working Britain experienced change as well:
with the men at war, it fell to the women of the country
to keep the factories going. Anthony Burton explores
that change.

978 0 7524 9886 7

Visit our website and discover many
other First World War books.

www.thehistorypress.co.uk/first-world-war